FAITH OF THE FATHERS

Science, Religion, and Reform in the

Development of Early American Sociology

William H. Swatos, Jr.

105171
Wyndham Hall Press
...a tradition of excellence...

FAITH OF THE FATHERS

Science, Religion, and Reform in the
Development of Early American Sociology

by

William H. Swatos, Jr.
Department of Sociology
Northern Illinois University

Library of Congress
Catalog Card Number
84-052863

ISBN 0-932269-11-7

TABLE OF CONTENTS

FOREWORD

During much of the twentieth century, American sociologists have tended to neglect, and even to belittle, their own native sociological forebears as unsophisticated Protestant churchmen intent on reforming society by means of Christian theology and morality. More than that, these early founders of our discipline, like Sumner, Small, Ward, Ely, Giddings and others, were considered intellectually inferior to the "great" European thinkers like Marx, Durkheim, Simmel, Toennies and Weber. In other words, our native progenitors could well be ignored while we paid reverence to the Europeans.

It is probably safe to say that by this time most graduate students and their professors pay scant attention to them, or shrug them off as denominational social workers. They are hardly mentioned in lectures and courses, and in contemporary textbooks. The author revives their memory at a time when the crucial issues of sociology are again being argued. We are now no longer so sure that sociology is, or should be, a **wertfrei** science. Some of our contemporaries are raising the kind of arguments that Sumner provoked when he said it was "an absurd effort to make the world over."

A significant aspect of this essay is the reminder that the early American sociologists did not fit the stereotype of the moralizing preacher. At this late date it probably does not matter that the founding fathers were not men of deep Christian faith and religious conviction. Some of them were indeed ordained clergymen but they were all essentially rationalists, or scientific humanists. Nor were they always in agreement among themselves. In fact, when Richard Ely established the American Institute of Christian Sociology, he was vigorously opposed by Albion Small, who founded the American Journal of Sociology as well as the first American Department of Sociology at the University of Chicago.

This is a timely study because it confronts two current tendencies that speak up in favor of social reform. The first is an informal group among some of the younger sociologists who are dissatisfied with the arid mathematical generalizations of strictly "scientific" sociology. They are tired of the system-builders who fail to confront the real world of social conflict. They want sociologists to be "for" something more than analytical theorizing. The second group of sociologists goes even further in the deliberate espousal of a so-called Christian perspective. In establishing the Christian Sociological Society they are not repudiating rationality and science. They want to make room for traditional Judeo-Christian values and insights alongside the current "naturalistic" approach to the study of social groups and relations.

Serious reflection on the **FAITH OF THE FATHERS** may help us to avoid excesses that appear to be both historical and contemporary. In other words, the complexity of socio-cultural systems is a perennial problem that challenges both faith and reason.

Joseph H. Fichter
Loyola University

PREFACE

This essay is an extension of work on the early years of American sociology that I presented in a similarly-titled article which was published in the Spring, 1983, issue of SOCIOLOGICAL ANALYSIS. Those portions that are reprinted here from that piece appear with the gracious permission of the Association for the Sociology of Religion. I am pleased to be able to bring this present edition to publication because it enables me both to correct some minor errors in the article and to enlarge especially upon the topic of Institutes of Christian Sociology. As the discipline of sociology becomes increasingly conscious of issues of value and application, the relationship of the field to other value-orientations takes on renewed importance. Unfortunately, treatments of this aspect of the profession's early history have been confusing and innacurate. If there is one thing worse than ahistorical sociology, it is sociology doing bad history. I hope that through a judicious use of both primary and secondary materials I have brought some integrity to this sub-topic.

My work in this area began in 1976, when Shannon Jung asked me to do something for a bicentennial lecture series on religion in American life at Virginia Intermont College, where he then taught. As the national bicentennial marked the centennial of sociological instruction in the United States as well, it seemed a natural topic. The editor of the JOURNAL OF THE HISTORY OF SOCIOLOGY would later comment, however, on how rare such observances actually were. In any case, I then presented the material at the annual meeting of the Society for the Scientific Study of Religion, whose members as always were generous with both support and criticism. A network grew up to include Benjamin Nelson, Toby Huff, Jeff Hadden, Myer Reed, Bob Perrin, and Tom Hood, to each of whom I owe a special debt.

A number of my students while I was at King College did yeoman service gathering preliminary materials, particularly Ada Jo Walton, and Jane Beebe of the Grinnell College library staff kindly searched their archives to provide materials on the summer Institute there. This essay might well still be in process, too, had it not been for the considerable research assistance rendered by Priscilla Swatos, the best librarian I'll ever marry. As a sociologist I am also aware of the institutional contexts involved in the completion of such a project. I am especially grateful to Northern Illinois University for providing the organizational environment that facilitated publication at this time.

This essay is dedicated to my children, Giles and Eric, who probably gave up the most while it was in preparation, and to James W. Gladden, my graduate school advisor and director, who had a genuine sensitivity to the religion-science-reform problematic, which even before I began this project made me suspicious of easy answers.

I

ON THE CONSTRUCTION OF A
SOCIOLOGICAL PAST IN AMERICA

Karl Marx, Emile Durkheim, and Max Weber command major attention in contemporary American sociology as the "Founding Fathers" of the discipline. Simmel, Spencer, Comte and perhaps Pareto round out the obvious patriarchy as grandfathers or uncles.[1] These are the names from the past most likely to be cited when looking for theoretical underpinnings or discussing the formation of the sociological consciousness.[2] Although there may be occasional references to Cooley, G.H. Mead, or Sumner, rare indeed is the mention of Lester Frank Ward, Albion W. Small, Franklin Giddings, E.A. Ross, or several other figures signally active in the development of sociology in America, as more than historical curiosities. Yet those who are cited and those who are not were all more or less contemporaries of one another. Whereas sociology continues to be primarily a North American discipline, even as it reaches the extremes of the globe, the general neglect of serious historical treatments of American theory is the more remarkable.[3] The question thus arises of what happened in the course of the development of American sociology to create a situation in which only symbolic interactionism of the myriad schools of sociological thought today is willing to trace its ancestry from American sources.[4] Why have the European thinkers come to be the major figures of the discipline, while the work of the Americans is largely glossed?

From introductory texts to scholarly articles, the literature of the history of sociology in America is replete with references to the Protestant Christian backgrounds and interests of the early Fathers as an apparent, though partial, explanation of their failure to persist as theorists of the new science. While the Schwendingers are the

1

most cautious in this regard, Smith tries to tie Christianity, sociology, and corporate capitalism into a causal chain. Hinkle and Hinkle speak of the "ministerial careers" of a covey of the early leaders, to which Oberschall also gives some credence, and Morgan argues that "the Social Gospel and early sociology were often indistinguishable in terms of both ideas and leading personnel."[5] Curiously, however, there has been very little careful examination of the nature of the underlying faith commitments of the Fathers or the dynamics of the relations of these to their sociology. Yet if their religiosity is of some relevance to their sociology--and so it must be assumed, given the extent of references to it--we must know more about it than we do. Why did the early American Fathers generally turn to reform and the academy rather than preaching and prayer meetings? Why did they think the church to be important even after they themselves largely moved to freethought or agnosticism? What **specifically** was the nature of their faith, and whence did it derive?

These are not simple questions to answer. There can be no doubt that almost to a man all of the early American Fathers professed and called themselves Christian. Their Christianity, however, was substantially at variance from that which has been held by the bulk of Christian believers in any era--including our own. Normative Christianity is theistic, supernatural, trinitarian, and more often than not adopts a relatively legalistic moral code. It manifests itself as biblical, creedal, and liturgical. Although forms of piety differ widely, these basic elements are stable. The Fathers, on the other hand, rejected virtually all of these. They were anti-theological, anti-legal, and anti-ritual. Their faith was naturalistic and consisted primarily of a progressivist-pragmatist application of the Golden Rule.[6] The roots of this belief-action system lay in (a) Comte's pious positivism (the "high priesthood" of sociologists);[7] (b) a generally communitarian reading of the Scottish Moralists which was consistent with that of Jefferson, for example, though not with

2

later nineteenth-century **laissez-faire** versions;[8] and (c) for most, a humanitarian evolutionism.[9] They shared elements of this faith with the Social Gospel movement, Christian Socialism, and liberal academic theology, all of which were somewhat congenitally intertwined. Though partially integrated into the life of many Christian bodies, this was not the dominant strand in Christian thought in its own time. The ultimate result, furthermore, was not the triumph of sociology as the "new science" for Christian living (replacing the old "science" of theology), but a gradual separation of sociology from church social action programs--as sociology increasingly defined itself as "pure" rather than applied science.[10]

From this vantage point, it is difficult to understand the emphasis placed upon the Fathers' Protestant Christian backgrounds. Their religion coincided much more with what might be termed "intellectual civil religion" than with Christian doctrine or practice. Though the words "Christian," "Christ," and "Jesus" occur in some of their writings in a postive way, the substantive content of these terms in relation to normative Christianity is virtually nil. The early Fathers were Protestant Christians because most American intellectuals of the nineteenth century were (at least nominally) Protestant Christians. Their "faith" reflected their culture. But their operating principles were those of scientific humanism. Christianity and the churches were part of a cultural mindset that gave the Fathers' thoughts specific **forms** of expression, but had little direct effect upon the **content** of their ideas. Put differently: had sociology flowered in an Islamic culture, for example, one would expect that its early leaders would come from Muslim backgrounds and express themselves in language forms derived from that culture, one element of which is clearly religious.

Theology as a discipline had been somewhat insecure since the late eighteenth century, but its greatest blows came with the tremendous scientific discoveries of the nineteenth. Dogmatics suddenly seemed very **passe,**

3

especially in centers of **learning.** As a result, theologians began to chart new courses for themselves and their students. Historicist biblical criticism, for example, was one possibility. Another was to try to deal in some responsible way with the problem of existence in industrial society. This meant an effort to salvage something out of Christianity that would improve the quality of life. Though doctrinal pronouncements might not be in order, the example of Jesus--how he lived among his fellows-- might be of great relevance to a world once again turned upside down. As one author phrased it, the "social revolution which seems to be immanent" is a good reason "why a minister should study sociology," for "in changed conditions of society he should be a leader."[11]

Two orientations toward this problem can be distinguished. One sought to get back to "real Christianity" or "the religion of Jesus" or "the practical application of Biblical truth" before organizational and dogmatic constraints polluted it. This can be found espoused more or less pietistically among many evangelical authors of the period well beyond the range of those who ever even came near dabbling in sociology. Ironically, it led to both liberalism and fundamentalism. The other approach was to move "beyond Christianity" (or the Bible) without thereby jettisoning everything associated with the old faith. This strand was obviously not capable of an alliance with fundamentalism. The various movements for **social** reform--as distinguished from, though not necessarily opposed to, individual salvation--that called themselves "Christian" at the turn of the century fused these two elements into relatively fragile, but flexible, structures of association. The Social Gospel leaders emphasized the first more heavily; the sociologists, the second. The Christian Socialists most mixed the two, hence their particularly ambiguous and enigmatic character as a movement.[12]

Like their Puritan forebears, the nineteenth-century liberal Protestants who were drawn to sociology sought, if not the holy commonwealth, at least the good society. Stung by their own past and present experience, however, they recognized that if they were to be heard to speak authoritatively, they had to work from this world. Empirical social conditions had to be known empirically; only then could theology speak in terms of practical ethics. But "theology" still carried the bad taste of dogmatics. **Sociology** was the scientific way of knowing (**episteme**) that provided the alternative to both Puritan and Marxist **gnosis**.[13] Sociology would reveal not what was above human knowing but what was available to human knowing, if we but knew the way to know. Science gave the **method** for access to this inner-worldly truth. The assumptions of the method, furthermore, had been justified theologically from the time of Aquinas forward, but particularly by the rationalistic theologians of the eighteenth century. Sociology thus provided a new context for testing Christian principles and putting those that survived to use. In this way, at least, sociology provided a "new gospel." Whereas Puritanism provided an inner-worldly ascetic based on other-worldly truth, sociology as the tool of liberal theologians would take the additional step of locating "saving" truth in this world as well.

However peculiar it may sound to today's reader, early American sociology had at one and the same time a scientific, reformist, and religious character. Symbolized best perhaps by the University of Chicago's seal featuring a phoenix rising out of the ashes--long a symbol of the new life of the Resurrection in Christian tradition, which had adapted it from the classics--with the motto **Crescat Scientia, Vita Excolatur** ("Let science grow that human life be enriched"), the discipline that had its real start at the newly revived university sought throughout its early years to provide empirical knowledge for right action. Typically American in its sense of practicality, the new science would seek to prove its truth on the basis of its usefulness. Because it **worked**, it would argue its superiority over traditional religious theories and remedies, being more capable of effecting the ethical principles of Christianity than Christianity (i.e., dogmatics) itself--and ethical principles were all that was left of Christianity in liberal Protestant circles by the turn of the twentieth century. Sociology was scientific in that it was empirical **and practical**--much of the paraphernalia of what today we would call "pure" science was referred to as "**philosophical** apparatus" on into the nineteenth century. Sociology was reformist in that it sought to make a better world for human life. And it was religious in that it recognized the function of shared values for the integration of society and sought to mobilize this insight through the already established--but in its own assessment, decadent -- social-organizational network of the churches.[14]

Although it would be a mistake to say that early American sociology was either un- or anti-Christian, it is also far too facile to label it "Christian," and let it go at that. Sociology was a new faith rooted in a particular socio-cultural reading of Judeo-Christian ethics that ultimately stood over against what the bulk of Christians then and now regard as the essential elements of their belief and practice.[15] This is not to suggest that the Founding Fathers ought to have embraced Christian orthodoxy--or contemporary practitioners of the discipline either, for that matter. To understand the history of sociology properly, however, we must be careful to specify what it is we mean when we apply our terms. As sociologists we should find particularly interesting the question of whether the early protagonists of the discipline were drawn to it because of "the general ethical tone of Christianity" that had seeped into nineteenth-century American culture or through causes uniquely situated in the religious institution or an interaction of both. This question in turn has sociology of knowledge implications that continue into the present day regarding the current and future relation of sociology to religion.[16] Early American sociology, too, was by no means a monolith. To imply that the Fathers shared a single viewpoint in everything would be foolhardy. By the same token, there were commonali-

6

ties between them sufficient to permit generalizations. The discipline itself clearly underwent a developmental process that was self-conscious and reflective. To say that two early sociologists were "former ministers," for example, in no way demonstrates that their involvement in sociology had the same goals or even intended to use the same means.

The remainder of this essay will be devoted to an examination of materials primarily drawn from the formative years of American sociology -- beginning in 1876 with Sumner's first course in sociology at Yale, and ending at 1925, the year of Albion Small's death. From these it will be seen that the religious orientations of the leading figures were complex and not necessarily consistent. The picture that emerges is by no means neat and tidy, but it does suggest that future treatments of the early American Fathers should approach references to their "Protestant" religious backgrounds and Christian interests with greater care. Perhaps much more important are their social class backgrounds and interests and the intersection of these with specific geo-historical settings.[17] From a comparative standpoint we might ask more questions than we have about the appearance of both Catholic and Jewish sociologies and sociologists. Were these reflective of the need to assert a different religious worldview, or did they reflect differences in class and status either in society as a whole or academe in particular (or both)? We would do well to heed here as elsewhere Peter Berger's sociological caution: "The first wisdom of sociology is this -- things are not what they seem."[18]

II

IN THE BEGINNING, SUMNER

Although his place among the patriarchs was eventually questioned by both Small and Ward because of his adherence to Spencerian **laissez-faire** principles, William Graham

7

Sumner was unquestionably the pioneer American sociologist. An Episcopalian clergyman, Sumner served in parochial settings from 1869 to 1872. From then until his retirement in 1909, only months before his death in 1910, he was Professor of Political and Social Science at Yale. Small reports that Sumner "rather early acquired the rank of a Yale tradition ... lecturing on what might be described as **the sort of opinions that ought to be held on things in general by a Yale man** ... [N]o one was supposed to have 'done' Yale as a gentleman should, without having taken at least one course with 'Billy' Sumner."[1] His most recent biographer, too, reports something of the same attitude from an eyewitness as Sumner had an honorary degree conferred upon him as he retired from both his alma mater and employer: "You should have seen Sumner get his degree! A simply terrific hand clapping burst out, the young fellows and old ones yelled and cheered, men waved hats even ... Phelps read a few words. Then he said, reading, **'always a radical'**. At that word the old man ... straightened his shoulders back like a shot ... The audience roared aloud with delight, actually yelled."[2]

Whether these recollections particuarly complement what sociologists think of themselves today, they certainly fail to suggest that Sumner was remembered for his piety. In short, it is naive to assume that simply because Sumner was ordained in 1869, he was thereafter and forever out to spread the "comfortable Gospel of Christ" as his career enlarged. The fact that Sumner **left** pastoral work to take a non-theological position at Yale, 'though his formal graduate training at Gottingen had been in Biblical studies, may suggest something of his own sense of marginality to the church. That he was never deposed from the ministry should not be interpreted to mean that he was revered as a churchman. The fact that he was a Spencerian, furthermore, would have made him intellectually unsuited to the Social Gospel movement. His precise ecclesiastical status notwithstanding, his own words are most to the point: "I never consciously gave up a religious belief. It was as if I had put my beliefs into a drawer, and when I opened it there was nothing there at all."[4]

Sumner introduced his course in sociology in an announcement of 1876. By 1880 he was embroiled in controvery over his use of Spencer's STUDY OF SOCIOLOGY, a book that he had not read until his years as a parish priest.[5] The editors of POPULAR SCIENCE MONTHLY--a magazine that was clearly pro-Spencer and gave considerable attention to early sociology--came to his defense in a statement entitled "Sociology and Theology at Yale College." Because of the temporal priority of this piece and the generality of its intended audience, it deserves substantial attention, not only for what inklings we get from it about Sumner, but also for the larger picture it gives of the nature of sociology at this time: "There is no mistaking the significance of the term **social science**," the authors argue. "It implies that human society is part of Nature to be studied by observation and induction, like the other parts of Nature, and to be pursued in conformity with established scientific method." They continue: "As in astronomy or in botany so in sociology, the inquirer has to observe and compare phenomena throughout the whole field ... and thus arrive at a connected and comprehensive body of natural laws which make up the truths of the science ..." They suggest that the Yale trustees, instead of choosing Sumner, "could easily have chosen a facile man for perfunctory work, ... but they sought and obtained a **throughgoing student of the subject, a man of intellectual force and independence** ...," for "the first allegiance of the man of science [i.e., Sumner] is to truth as it is determined by the processes of reason, and ... he is bound to make no terms with preconceived erroneous opinions."

The core of the problem was a chapter of Spencer's SOCIOLOGY entitled "The Theological Bias," which "was considered by some of the faculty so objectionable as to render the volume unfit ..." for use at Yale. The editors

9

retort:

"If there is a bias from theolgoical influences that is calcu-
lated to vitiate or pervert the judgment upon social questions, what could be more important than that it should
be pointed out? In dealing with society from a scientific
point of view, Mr. Spencer had to consider it in its widest
relations ... Mr. Spencer, therefore, drew his illustrations
of the distorting influence of theological beliefs upon
views of society from different quarters. Mohammedans
and Feejeeans, Catholic and Protestant Christians, are
cited to exemplify the common tendencies of theological
doctrine to obscure the mental vision and prejudice opinion.

The difference in the points of view of the theologian
and the scientist comes out here sharply. Science inquires
into the laws of phenomena; social science into the laws
of social phenomena. As societies have developed, religious systems have also grown up as a part of the general
phenomena of social growth. Social science is concerned
with religion as a universal fact of human nature, which
gives rise to universal effects--it deals, in short, with
the natural laws of universal religious phenomena. With
these views theology has no sympathy. It is scornfully
and passionately rejected by the religious devotee. His
position is that there is one religion that is absolutely
true, and that all other relgions are absolutely false,
and any notion of treating them all alike is rejected
with horror."

The result of this opposition between sociological and
religious worldviews was "a storm of denunciation against
the sociologist and all his books, and the professor, faculty,
and college" in the religious press, for "religious prejudices
are stimulated to their utmost by the **odium theologicum.**"[6]

Discussions of the ultimate value of Spencer's sociology
are not particularly germane at this juncture. The significant point is that although Sumner may have been a
clergyman, his impact was not only anti-theological

10

in the narrow disciplinary sense, but also anti-church in the general common sense. He came across not as an apostle of Christianity but as an apostle of **science**, and the popular notion of the two was clearly different. He was, indeed, teaching a "new gospel" and was being cursed for it.[7] That he also recognized this is made strikingly clear in his Presidential Address to the American Sociological Society in December of 1909. His health was failing, and he had already retired from Yale. As it turned out, this was to be his last public presentation: his ultimately fatal stroke occurred while in New York for the meeting. He chose as his topic "Religion and the Mores." Three years before the publication of the ELEMENTARY FORMS, his words nevertheless represented what today might be termed a brilliant synthesis of Durkheim and Marx. There was also a disarming insightfulness about both his own worldview and the subject matter of our inquiry in his conclusion:

"... [R]eligion comes out of the mores and is controlled by them ... For an example, we may note how the humanitarianism of modern mores has colored and warped Christianity. Humanitarianism grew out of economic power by commerce, inventions, steam, and electricity. Humanitarianism led to opposition to slavery, and to the emancipation of women. These are not doctrines of the Bible or of Middle-Age Christianity. They were imposed on modern religion by the mores. Then they came from the religion to the modern world as religious ideas and duties, with religious and ecclesiastical sanctions. This is the usual interplay of the mores and religion."[8]

III

INSTITUTES OF CHRISTIAN SOCIOLOGY

The shores of Lake Chautauqua, New York, formed the site for what has come to be known as the "Chautauqua

Movement." Started in 1874 by Methodist Bishop John H. Vincent (the father of George E. Vincent, one of Small's later colleagues and collaborators at Chicago), for the preparation of church Sunday school teachers, "the movement rapidly became the most important national instrument for adult education," and traveling "Chautauquas" soon swept the nation. In 1887 William Rainey Harper-- Yale divine, principal of the College of Liberal Arts at Chautauqua, and soon-to-be president of the Rockefeller-revived University of Chicago, the man who would invite Albion Small to inaugurate the first full-fledged department of sociology in the country--asked Richard T. Ely to join the summer and extension faculty.[1] A noted economist on the faculty of John Hopkins University, Ely numbered among his graduate students such figures of future importance as Frederick Jackson Turner, John R. Commons, E.A. Ross, Albion Small, and Woodrow Wilson. He also was active in the Christian Socialist movement, seeing in it the only possible resolution of the continuing rifts in the social order created by class struggles. Simply put, he accepted Marx's analysis of the current social problem, but not his solution.

Ely lectured widely on the Christian "middle way" between revolutionary socialism--popularly termed "anarchism"-- and **laissez-faire** capitalism. His books THE SOCIAL ASPECTS OF CHRISTIANITY (1889) and THE SOCIAL LAW OF SERVICE (1896) became standards for Protestant social reformers. For over twenty years Methodist seminarians were required to read the former, as well as his INTRODUCTION TO POLITICAL ECONOMY. The Epworth Youth League of the Methodist church placed THE SOCIAL LAW OF SERVICE on its required reading list. His books also appeared on the required reading list for United Brethren seminarians and were almost universally studied by branches of the Anglican and Protestant Episcopal Christian Social Union. Progressive college professors sent their advanced ministerial students directly to Ely for training in the social sciences. "Unto whom should I send them if not to you?," George Herron of Iowa College

(Grinnell) once asked Ely rhetorically.[2] The essence of Ely's message, moreover, was amazingly simple; namely, that Christ's second commandment ("Love thy neighbor ..."), "in its elaboration, becomes social science or sociology."[3] Thus Small describes Ely as the "founder of the 'Christian Sociology' movement."[4]

It was in this context that Ely enlisted the aid of Herron at Chautauqua in the summer of 1893 to form the American Institute of Christian Sociology.[5] Ely was elected president. Bishop Vincent headed a list of five clerical vice-presidents. Commons served as secretary, and Herron was named "principal of instruction and organization" or lecturer.[6] Commons would later describe his participation as a "venture outside of the academic field."[7] Membership was open to all. The objects were threefold:

1. To claim for the Christian law the ultimate authority to rule social practice;
2. To study in common how to apply the principles of Christianity to the social and economic difficulties of the time;
3. To present Christ as the living Master and King of men, and His kingdom as the complete ideal of human society to be realized on earth.

The work of the group was envisioned to include:

"...[T]he publication of papers which relate to Christian sociology, the recommendation of courses of reading, the preaching of sermons and delivery of addresses on sociological topics ..., the formation of local institutes for study and practical work, the encouragement of the study of social science by founding libraries, scholarships, fellowships, lectureships and professorships, and annual conventions of the general body."[8]

Two open meetings were to be held. The first, at Grinnell, promised addresses from Ely, Herron, Commons, Josiah Strong, and Graham Taylor, who held the chair of Christian

13

Sociology at Chicago Theological Seminary. Ulysses Grant Weatherly--Commons' colleague at Indiana University and a subsequent president of the American Sociological Society--also joined the group.[9]

Ely, however, never went to the meetings. He was dissuaded from doing so by a series of letters from none other than his former Hopkins student, Chicago sociology department chairman Albion Small, who derided Herron's sociology as "unsafe, unfactual and dogmatic." Herron and his colleague George Gates (Grinnell's president), Small wrote, disgust "every man of my acquaintance," and their sociology, he warned Ely, "is essentially ... a repudiation of your own method of making sure of the facts before offering to preach programs." He argued that the Institute would be "likely to do incalculable harm if it is to turn loose on innocent searchers for social truth a raft of untrained social physicians with a sociological faith cure"; thus Small's final admonition: "In so far as you encourage and tacitly endorse that unscholarly and illiberal course ... you must necessarily forfeit a measure of confidence."[10] Indeed, when Ely wrote his autobiography in 1938, he had fond words for Chatauqua, but nothing to say about the Institute.[11] He did make the Chautauqua meetings in 1894, but there resigned any connection with the Institute's activities, for two interconnected reasons. First, he was placed on the defensive with regard to his own "radicalism" by an attacking university trustee. He survived the battle, but in the process began something of a "retreat from reform" into more "objective" academic work.[12] In the meantime, the Grinnel meeting had taken place, with many being shocked by Herron's unabashed socialism and unremitting anti-capitalism. Caught in the press, Ely's cause was not particularly favored by an association with Herron; although Herron and Gates for their part offered Ely both moral support through his ordeal and a position at Grinnell if he should not be victorious. During and after the trial, however, Ely turned down offers to come to Grinnell either as lecturer or more permanently.[13]

14

Many of the participants at the Grinnell meeting had gathered in 1893 in Chicago for the Congress of the Evangelical Alliance for the United States, which was held to coincide with the World's Fair there. It produced a set of essays, CHRISTIANITY PRACTICALLY APPLIED, which indicates something of the breadth of interest in Christian Sociology. Commons attended both the summer conferences and some Chicago lectures by Herron, whom he terms "an eminent minister of the Gospel," but Commons

"...became upset as to the meaning of Christian Socialism and Christian Sociology. On one night of his series our lecturer identified Christianity with pure Anarchism; on the next night he identified it with Communism. He identified each with the love of God. But I now became mystified on the meaning of Love itself. I could not make out whether Christian Socialism meant Love of Man or Love of Woman. On this issue our Institute of Christian Sociology split and disappeared."[14]

Stern adds the observation that Herron, "incurred the wrathful protests of the clergy against his criticisms of capitalism through the medium of the organization, although these criticisms were merely based on an evaluation of capitalism in terms of 'Christian ethics' without reference to a political program."[15] Herron's basic arguments on these points are set out in his books THE CHRISTIAN SOCIETY (1894) and THE CHRISTIAN STATE (1895). One reviewer, more positively disposed than Small or Commons, writes that Herron's "message ... is the logic of Ely, Strong and Commons on fire," and adds regarding the Institute, "to judge from the literary vigor of its leading spirits, [it] is not likely to lack in vitality as it widens the circle of its influence."[16] Instead the intensity of the flames consumed the structure.

1894 also saw an attempt at another Christian sociological endeavor. This was the Oberlin Institute of Christian

Sociology, whose organizer was Z. Swift Holbrook, author of THE LESSONS OF THE HOMESTEAD TROUBLES (1892), "a Chicago businessman and academic adventurer whose star shone briefly at Oberlin," who "deplored the sentimentalism, the 'altruistic tendency', which he asserted marked the thinking" of some academic and religious sociologists--specifically, George Herron. He was initiallly brought to Oberlin by George Frederick Wright, a professor in the theological seminary noted most for his contributions to geology, who had moved to Ohio a decade earlier from a Congregationalist pastorate in Andover, Massachusetts, soon also bringing the editorship of the journal BIBLIOTHECA SACRA, one of the nation's oldest, semi-independent theological journals. Holbook's name was added as co-editor in 1894 as well, and by 1895 a subtitle was added to the masthead: A REGLIOUS AND SOCIOLOGICAL QUARTERLY.[17] Oberlin had been very sympathetic to both the social sciences and the Social Gospel. The Reverend Washington Gladden, a leader in the latter, became pastor of the First Congregational Church in Columbus in 1882. By 1896, he was on the college's Board of Trustees. Ely, Lyman Abbott, John Bascom, and J.H.W. Stuckenberg--each of whom had written some form of Christian Sociology text--all had been speakers on the campus. John Commons, who completed his undergraduate work there, spent his first year of teaching at the college, and proposed new methods of instruction. One actually initiated by his successor, J. William Black, was that of bringing outside speakers of differing viewpoints into class. This strategy underlay the Oberlin Institute of Christian Sociology.[18]

The first meeting of the Institute occurred in November. Strong, Taylor, Stuckenberg, and Gladden, who was elected president, were present. Also in attendance was a young Oberlin English professor on leave that term to study sociology at Chicago: W.I. Thomas. The clergy spoke to relatively standard Social Gospel themes, while Holbrook and Thomas sparred on the nature of sociology. The former argued for "in effect, a sociology that would contain whatever one wished to uphold," while Small's graduate student advocated "careful, objective observation and strict scientific reasoning ... The scientific sociologist ... could furnish the only sure guidance in the tasks of reform. Any body of doctrine with less secure foundations would be only a receptacle for personal or class interest." This was apparently Thomas' sole contact with the Institue, and he makes no mention of it in autobiographical materials.[19]

The major task of this fall meeting, however, was to prepare for a "Summer School of Christian Sociology" in 1895 at the college. The topic was "The Causes and Proposed Remedies for Poverty." Unique to the plan was an intention that representatives of both labor and ownership would be present. A variety of notable speakers appeared: John Bates Clark, Clarence Darrow, Jane Addams, Samuel Gompers, the United States Commissioner of Labor, and several business executives. A contemporary observer thought the Oberlin Institute "worthy of special commendation and imitation because labor leaders were there brought face to face with Christian capitalists and pastors in friendly conference."[20] Apparently the capitalists were not sufficiently impressed: despite plans to make the Summer School an annual event, it was terminated after this single session for lack of adequate financial support.

A most interesting byproduct of this effort, however, was a piece of empirical research by Holbrook to solicit opinions from academicians, clergy, government officials, and others on the "propriety of the term 'Christian Sociology'." From an unstated number of inquiries, 126 postal card responses were received and printed in full in BIBLIOTHECA SACRA.[21] One category of reply was that represented by a now frequently cited statement of Ward's: "I am in the habit of considering Sociology to be a science, not a religion, cult, or programme of action and therefore

'Christian Sociology' sounds to me about as would Christian Mathematics, Mohammedan Biology, or Buddhist Chemistry. If it is no better than Christian Astronomy, Geology, and Geography used to be in the days when such things were recognized, it is a rather poor article." This was by no means an isolated remark. The President of M.I.T., for example, wrote: "If **Sociology** is a name given **to a science,** then the expression 'Christian Sociology' is as improper as would be the title 'Christian Geometry' or 'Christian Thermodynamics'." Indeed, if we remember that these comments were solicited simultaneously and independently, perhaps the strongest testimony to the ready acceptance of this point of view by 1895 is that Herron, in one of the longest responses in the whole group, chose to address it and it alone:

"The recent dogma that there can be no Christian science of society any more than a Christian astronomy or a Christian biology is as unworthy of respect as intellectual honesty can make it ... Christianity has not been the chief force and fact in the development of the toad, the star, the plant, the rock ...
[T]here has been no volition, no choice, no morality, in the development of the plant, the rock, the animal. It was not by faith in a certain person, or in certain principles, that the rock became the kind of rock it is ...
Society is the creation of the forces which issue from the faiths of the people. The interpretation of these forces, with some judgment of their effect upon present economies and institutions ... is the first service not only of the Christian apostle, but of any true science of society ..."

Yet Herron was Holbrook's problem. In a separate piece he wrote: "Professor Herron has been weighed in the balances and found wanting. How such a mind found its way into the class room must remain a mystery, for the emotions, spasms, and shrieks have no more merit because they play on the word 'Jesus' than if they shouted 'Great is Diana of the Ephesians,' or 'Hosanna to the

Son of David,' or 'Crucify him'."[22] Thus his heart should have been warmed by Small's response--one of the most vitriolic in the series and clearly directed against Herron. "I object to the phrase 'Christian Sociology'," he writes,

"because it seems to me either pleonastic or fraudulently pretentious ... [I]t is offensive both to taste and morals in the airs which men give themselves under its shelter. I object to its use to conceal ignorance of social facts and the processes by which ignorance must be informed. I object to it as a device for dignifying incompetence and laziness. I object to the humbuggery of reading one's personal opinions into the New Testament, and then reading them out again in the name of Christ. Sociology is not a substitute for Christian truth, but it is a body of inquiries about subjects which the New Testament does not expound any more than it elaborates Physics or Chemistry or the theory of medicine. A man who has no special knowledge of society no more deserves to rank as a prophet for calling himself a "Christian Sociologist" than any other species of ignoramus would be entitled to a teacher's certificate by distinguishing himself as a 'Christian Ignoramus'."

Small, then, went too far for Holbrook's tastes in another direction. He had, after all, already published an article on "Christian Sociology" in an earlier issue of BIBLIO-THECA SACRA and remained committed to the rather vague concept articulated there. The tide was clearly turning against him, however. Though his friend Stuckenberg, who had written a book explicitly titled CHRISTIAN SOCIOLOGY in 1880, answered the query by saying that, "Whatever opposition the term 'Christian Sociology' may meet with, it is evidently here to remain," the weight of opinion was otherwise.[23] Holbrook became more agitated and threatened his opposition in 1896:

"The study of sociology, as a science, will be confined to narrow lines and to few people, if Christian ideals and forces are not reckoned with ... The New Testament conception of society as it is, as it ought to be, and what will make it so, will then leave courses in scientific sociology so far behind in numbers and interest that they will practically drop out of sight, and sociology will then be spoken of as a passing fad. We predict the article 'The Passing of Sociology,' not long hence."[24]

In the United States, at least, the opposite was entirely the case.

Within two years' time, then, the Institues of Christian Sociology had virtually vanished. Herron continued to preach his radical Christian socialism, became involved in an unseemly marital affair, and ultimately settled in Italy--where he would, however, do diplomatic service during World War I for one of the old Hopkins' crowd he so much admired, the Professor-President Wilson. Ely, apparently shaken by his "trial" and by the treatment of two of his former students in similar cases who were not so fortunate, increasingly occupied himself with more explicitly professional concerns at the University of Wisconsin, where he sought to organize a department of "western" economists more congenial to his socio-political thinking. These would further bolster his position in the American Economic Association which he had founded in 1885 to counter the **laissez-faire**-dominated economics section of the American Historical Association, and subsequently have enormous impact on American political economics in both theory and practice. He was also unhappy to find himself dropped from the Chautauqua faculty in 1895, as he had understook his position there to be permanent. Indeed, the only article on sociology carried by THE CHAUTAUQUAN, that organization's semi-official magazine, during the whole period of the Institues was one by Albion Small, who addressed methodological concerns and made no mention of Christian Sociology.[25] John Commons spent only the years 1893 to 1895 at Indiana before moving to Syracuse, and then in succession to the federal government

20

and Ely's department, becoming the premier labor historian of his generation. Weatherly was more of an Indiana institution, working through departments of history and economics before settling into sociology, whence he became the national professional association president in 1923 and author of a functionalist treatise on social change. Holbrook's lecture career at Oberlin ended rather quickly after the Summer School plan failed to be per-petuated, though he remained co-editor of BIBLIOTHECA SACRA, which was independent of the college, until his death in 1900. The subtitle that was added when he came on, however, was maintained even beyond Wright's editorship, to be changed in 1934 to A THEOLOGICAL QUARTERLY.[26]

In the aftermath of the Herron incident, the Reverend Leander T. Chamberlain of New York had assumed some leadership of the American Institute of Christian Sociology and "toured the country on behalf of a reorganization of the society along more academic lines," including a project to "issue a journal for the publication of articles on sociology." Small was initially sympathetic to Chamber-lain's efforts for the Institue, which he too says Herron "practically wrecked," and even wrote to Ward that:

"Dr. Chamberlain ... is not at all misled by the term **Chris-tian** S'y., and would prefer to drop the epithet [!], but on the whole it seems likely to make more trouble than it would avoid. I feel like giving Dr. C. all the support I can, although I have my serious doubts about the consti-tuency which can be gathered, and about the results that can be reached. The aim is to make the **Churches** more effective social factors. The Herron faction imagines that the main reliance is the glorification of Christian sentiments. The majority understand with more or less distinctness that intelligence about social forces is the primary consideration, and they therefore want to build on Scientific Sociology."[27]

Small thus seemed for a moment to encourage the Chris-

21

tian Sociology effort, but not without a peculiar juxtaposition of the terms "Christian" and "scientific." What Small backed, then, was not the faith of these men and women but their ability to organize the churches as instruments for the dispersal and application of scientific knowledge.

Chamberlain, meanwhile, apparently reassessed the amount of trouble dropping "Christian" would cause, for there shortly appeared an announcement in the ANNALS as follows:

"**American Institute of Sociology.** That organization, formerly known as the American Institute of Christian Sociology, has recently been reorganized on a broader and more scientific basis, which will enable workers in all lines of sociological effort and representing all shades of belief to combine in a really effective national organization."

Its joint objects would be "to investigate the facts concerning society as a whole," and "to promote the use of all available truth for the betterment of society's condition to the end of the highest individual, domestic and collective well-being." No definite work of the new group had "yet been officially outlined," but an annual meeting was proposed. The ANNALS adds editorially, "There is certainly room for such an organization in America, and its efficiency and opportunities for usefulness can hardly be overestimated."[28]

Small's opposition to the "Herron faction," his lingering doubts about their real commitments--were they sentimental or scientific--and perhaps some prodding from Chicago president Harper ultimately carried the day. He dealt the movement an organizational deathblow only a month after his letter to Ward by publishing the AMERICAN JOURNAL OF SOCIOLOGY without any consultation with or positive reference to Chamberlain's effort, an assessment Chamberlain himself made in a subsequent letter to Ward.[29] Small's defence was that he was rushed into the publication by "the trustees of our University," but a comment in his initial editorial essay reveals both his predicament and resolve. He admits that "many" in his potential audience will consider the attitude of the new publication towards Christian Sociology "the most important question" to be addressed--a clear sign of the salience of the topic at the time. "The answer," he replies, "is, in a word, towards Christian sociology sincerely deferential, towards alleged 'Christian sociologists' severly suspicious." Small effectively undermined Christian Sociology by reducing its concerns to **ad hominem** arguments. This was a very different course from English Christian Sociology, for example, though both had common roots in Christian Socialism.[30] It should not go unnoticed, either, that Small wrote his vitriolic response to Holbrook's survey, his mild endorsement of Chamberlain's effort, and this piece of editorial tergiversation within a very few months of each other.[31]

The Christian Sociology movement in the United States largely died aborning. Even the Reverend Chamberlain's efforts to secularize its style waned before the onrush of academic institutions and their implied credibility. But what was it that was conceived in the first place? What was "Christian Sociology"? In Holbrook's survey, Stuckenberg takes credit for first introducing the term in his book by that title and claims rather blandly that "Christian Sociology aims to give the philosophy of Christian Society."[32] But when the writings of its proponents-- Ely, Commons, John Bascom, Herron for a period, and others--are examined today, the movement appears to have been the result of an effort to find a name for something they were trying to do in relating the churches to social problems as these leaders became increasingly uncomfortable about the connotations of Christian **Socialism.** Commons says quite directly that the American Institute of Christian Sociology "was organized ... to support an American version of what had been known in Europe as Christian Socialism,"[33] and by the time Ely wrote SOCIALISM AND SOCIAL REFORM (1894), for example, it was evident that he was sensitive to the tendency of Americans to identify socialism with anarchism and violent revolution. That he wanted to avoid this interpretation and implicit accusation--as he did the notion of a **communist** society, whether based on the principles of Marx or Jesus--is abundantly clear. The confusion and ambiguity that surrounded both the movement and the term Christian Socialism urged Ely to suggest that it was "perhaps best to drop the use of the expression." Christian **Sociology**, by contrast, was intended to emphasize the scientific knowledge-through-method character of Ely's commitment--his drive for "clear ideas ... accuracy ... clearness of thought ... some clear explanation"--and ease away from the political rhetoric of which socialism was so much a part in the late nineteenth century.[34]

A similar concern appears to lie behind such works as Bascom's SOCIOLOGY (1887), which on the one hand is nothing more than a scholarly statement of the Social Gospel's movement's "Kingdom theology," but on the other reflects an unwillingness to let a wall be built between social science and Christian faith. Indeed, when Bascom responded to Holbrook's survey, he rejected the phrase **Christian** Sociology because he felt it threatened the unity of knowledge under God's sovereignty. The same can be said for Commons' SOCIAL REFORM AND THE CHURCH (1894), which advances the novel thesis that Christianity is the "cause" of modern social problems, because it is Christian values themselves which create awareness of the evils of modernity. Even Stuckenberg's book can be read in this way, although it was to this trend that Ward would later raise some of his objections. If these men had had their way, Christian Sociology might have been **episteme**--a means of knowing by which the church could deal with the world, something even Small would have supported. But Christian Sociology in this context failed, ultimately splitting into revolutionary or gnostic forms. Neither of these was congenial to the academy, which remained throughout the primarly locus for the development of sociology.

Ely had an institutional commitment to the church as a complement to his conviction about the value of the new science and as an outcome of his own sociocultural milieu. At the time of his academic trial he wrote:

"As far as my general social philosophy is concerned ... I am a conservative rather than a radical, and in the strict sense of the term an aristocrat rather than a democrat; but when I use the word 'aristocrat,' I have in mind of course not a legal aristocracy, but a natural aristocracy ... an aristocracy which lives for the fulfillment for special service." [35]

At the same time that Ely was withdrawing from the American Institute of Christian Sociology for more mainline channels of academic influence, however, he did not abandon his religious conscience; rather, he returned to the narrower line of the work of the Episcopal Church he had chosen during his student years. The same issue of the ANNALS that reports Chamberlain's reformation of the Institute announces immediately thereafter a revival of the Christian Social Union. The president was New York's Bishop Henry C. Potter, among the vice-presidents was Professor Richard T. Ely, and its **membership was restricted to Episcopalians.** A clear line was now drawn between Ely's secular endeavors as an economist and his church life.

The objects of this reconstituted group have a familiar ring:

"First, to claim for the Christian law the ultimate authority to rule social practice; second, to study in common how to apply the moral truths and principles of Christianity to the social and economic difficulties of the present time; third, to present Christ in practical life as the leading Master and King, the enemy of wrong and selfishness, the power of righteousness and love."[36]

The first repeats the Institute's platform word-for-word; the second, substantially. Only the third shows marked deviation, and it is clearly in a conservative direction away from the "realized eschatology" of the Chautauqua formulary. It was also more consistent with Episcopalian teaching and Ely's own belief that the state was of divine institution. Most significant of all, however, is that this last phrase matches that printed in moderate Social Gospel leader Lyman Abbott's periodical, the OUTLOOK, for what the principles of the American Institute would be **prior to** its actual founding.[37]

Commons work shows similar tendencies. In his "Popular Bibliography of Sociology," written during his Oberlin teaching years of 1892 with special application to "the Christian minister and worker," for example, Commons mentions under the heading "Remedies," Marx's CAPITAL (The 'Bible of Socialism'"), Booth's IN DARKEST ENGLAND AND THE WAY OUT (the Salvation Army plan), two books by Washington Gladden, but saves his highest praise ("The best"), for C.M. Woodward's THE MANUAL TRAINING SCHOOL, a clearly liberal-technocratic and non-theological work. Commons' SOCIAL REFORM AND THE CHURCH is likewise an explicit admonition to denominational Christianity--and ministers especially--to heed the new knowledge and apply it or else face extinction as both organizations and credible social functionaries:

"I became suspicious of Love as the basis of social reform. I visited the Amana Community of Christian Communists in Iowa. They distinguished rigidly between love of man and love of woman. I studied Mazzini, the great Italian leader of Christian Socialism ... He founded Christian Socialism on the Duties of Man, including duties to wife and family. Eventually, after many years, in working out my institutional economics, I made Duty and Debt,

26

instead of Liberty and Love, the foundations of institutional economics."[38]

No significant figure calling himself or herself a sociologist
after 1900--except perhaps Weatherly, whose work was
not major nor his association with the Institutes clear--had
been related to the Christian Sociology movement in
America or the Institutes in any positive way.   They
were an attempt to clarify and respond to Christian
Socialism, and perhaps seen in that light they did tease
out and define some issues of significance. Except as
a **via negativa**, however, they cannot be said to have
made an important contribution to American sociological
theory nor to explain why American sociological theory
from the formative years remains neglected.

IV

SMALL AND WARD

Both Albion Small and Lester Frank Ward stood against
the pessimism of Sumner and for an optimistic humanistic
sociology.   Both also had religious intersts, but neither
could be termed orthodox. Small studied theology here
and abroad. He rejected a career in the ministry, however,
for an academic career in sociology. To speak of Small's
"ministerial career" thus exaggerates a phase of his education, for the closest he ever came to this was membership
in the board of deacons of a Baptist congregation in
Chicago, largely an honorific office. Ward--termed
by one biographer "The American Aristotle" and memorial-
ized along with 174 other "famous Americans" in the
kneelers of St. John's Chapel of Washington's National
Cathedral--spent almost his entire life in government
service, primarily as a geologist (though holding degrees
or diplomas in medicine, law, and botany). The first
edition of his principal work, DYNAMIC SOCIOLOGY,

27

was published with some assistance from Youmans of POPULAR SCIENCE MONTHLY, but at his own expense and with very limited circulation. Small nevertheless had great admiration for Ward and sought his friendship. A thoroughgoing Comtean with regard to the nature and place of sociology in the world of ideas, Ward claimed that Comte's hierarchy was "the most sublime, interesting, and important idea of the nineteenth century."[1] In an article written at Small's request for the first issue of the A.J.S.--which paid non-University of Chicago contributors at that time--Ward likewise termed sociology "the last and highest of the sciences ... the cap sheaf and crown of any true system of classification of the sciences, and the last and highest landing on the great staircase of education."[2]

Ward had a passion for education, and by his late teens he had already developed a negative reaction to organized religion. This occurred well before any acquaintance with sociology. "Ward's secularization," a modern biographer writes, "had its origins ... in the strong wave of evangelical Protestant resistence to the influx of Catholicism ... [S]cience did not so much subvert his belief, but that theology itself kept him from becoming an adherent of the reigning orthodoxy; for only later was science accepted by him as an alternate faith."[3] After a Civil War injury, Ward settled in Washington and there founded the National Liberal Reform League in 1869 and edited from 1870 to 1871 its publication, THE ICONOCLAST. League members agreed to "unite upon the cardinal principles of hostility to the leading doctrinal teachings of the so-called Catholic and evangelical Protestant Churches, and of zeal for the triumph of reason and science over faith and theology." His first major article, "The New Faith," appeared as the opening piece in the fledgling journal, and overall he wrote 65 editorials and articles that "analyzed specific doctrines of orthodoxy and reported present and past misdeeds and the dogmatism of theology." During this same period, Ward tried many churches, and ultimately settled upon a Unitarian congregation, which he attended infrequently but supported financially throughout his life.[4]

In later years, Ward returned to his religious interests and gave his hand to "attempts to work out a philosophic basis for a world religion freed from superstition." He jotted down the title for, but never wrote, an essay on "Monism the True Quietism, or the Continuity of Nature the only Faith that can satisfy the emancipated Soul." His early biographer and sometime colleague, James Q. Dealy, claims that Ward was "deeply religious, not theologically or ecclesiastically, but in the idealism of his morals and his aspiration to make achievements helpful to humanity." While rebelling against "theology in all its forms," he professed a "Gospel of Science" and believed strongly that his "sociological teachings would make possible a more rapid rate of human progress." To this end he "preached the gospel of equal opportunity that each might attain the best of which he was capable," at the same time as he stood in awe before the mysteries of nature.[5]

Ward himself dealt with prevailing religious questions and criticisms by claiming: "If it is truth it may come from a carpenter of Nazareth or from an attic in the Latin Quarter; sooner or later all the world will accept it."[6] Ward thus advanced sociology as the keystone of a new scientistic gnosticism, and this as the cure for the world's ills. Since the new gnosticism had the Truth, whatever in Christianity coincided with that truth could be retained. "I am the Way, the Truth, and the Life," was turned on its ear. Sociological **knowledge** provided the canon for truth, not biblical revelation or church dogmatics. Ward's faith in science, knowledge, and education was to him but an acknowledgement of "reality," though we may interpret it from our vantage point in terms of the causes of religion and reform. In his own eyes, Ward was neither a heretic nor a visionary, but a realist. In any case, we can see here the clear discontinuity between his faith and prevailing forms of Christian belief and practice.

Small's admiration for Ward rested primarily on the fact that DYNAMIC SOCIOLOGY effectively refuted the biologically-based Spencer-Sumner evolutionary scheme and the **laissez-faire** economics that proceeded from it, but his esteem did not end there. Had Small wanted a non-Sumnerian reference only, he could have turned to Bascom's SOCIOLOGY, already well-know to Christian social reformers and a much more popular work than Ward's. What Small admired in Ward's book especially was that it provided a "naturalistic" basis for understanding purposive human action. Ward was, after all, a **bona fide** scientist. Small widely recommended Ward's work and adopted his organicism into Small and Vincent's INTRODUCTION TO THE STUDY OF SOCIOLOGY, which became the standard text.[7] That Small honored Ward's judgment is perhaps best demonstrated by the fact that it was he who convinced Small--albeit grudgingly--that Sumner ought to be the second president of the American Sociological Society (after Ward, whom Small essentially handpicked). Ward's arguments for a sense of the history of the profession as a science--something to which Small was obviously committed--won out over the value of the liberal humanism which both also shared.

The careers of the two men on the other hand obviously diverged. Ward was a government scientist; Small an academician and administrator--first at his alma mater Colby, where he rose to be president, then at Chicago. Small thus had to deal with a rather different constituency than Ward. Although it may be unfair to label Small "Machiavellian," there can be little doubt that he lived with a realistic sense of his own importance to both sociology and the university, and that part of this was based upon his ability to choose his words with discretion and react situationally. Small was "a leading figure in the struggle of sociology to achieve professional academic status as a science," and he recognized early on that "the future of sociology as a discipline depended upon the discovery of an appropriate institutional form for its exercise."[8]

30

Out of this combination of factors, the private correspondence from Small to Ward takes on special significance for our understanding of Small's appeal to Christianity in some of his public statements.[9] Together they do much to prove, as Dibble has remarked, that "Small was not a preacher's kid who had never been weaned."[10]

The concern throughout this series is Ward's treatment of religion in DYNAMIC SOCIOLOGY. Small's interest, however, is not for religious truth, but the possibility that Ward may alienate a potential public for the new knowledge of sociology. The first letter is dated September 18, 1890, just as Small is beginning to offer sociology at Colby. He had read Ward but decided to issue his own text for the courses. In it he stated that the "tendency of sociology must be towards an approximation of the ideal of social life contained in the Gospels,"[11] a language-form that he was soon to deemphasize in professional work, but which he thought necessary to win his audience. To Ward he writes that he is "unable to sympathize with many of your views, especially on religious relations," and he regrets that Ward expressed his opinion "so freely on religious subjects, for on that account many are willing to throw aside you volumes entirely, whereas, without injury to the course of thought, the omission of these references would have left such persons no occasion for suspicion of your methods."[12]

Ward replied sharply that he "did not write for the feeble minded" and that his purpose was not to seek popularity in any case. Writing October 3, 1890, Small answered that he feared he had not made himself "perfectly clear" in his earlier remarks regarding Ward's comments on religion: "**Simply from the strategic or rhetorical point of view**," Small continues, he regrets that Ward did not refrain "from certain details which, whatever their importance in the argument, necessarily shock certain people ..." Not as a matter of popularlity, "but for the sake of **spreading discoveries of the truth**," it is "wiser to understate, in order not to frighten away the feeble minded, than to express one's self in full ..." Small claims: "There are thousands of men who hold to the substance of the traditional evangelical doctrines, who are yet theoretically willing to be convinced that any one of them is untenable ... [I]t is better in dealing with such men ... to adopt Beecher's advice, 'Don't let too many cats out of the bag at once'."[13]

In January of 1893, Small wrote to Ward as the result of reviewing his PSYCHIC FACTORS IN CIVILIZATION. Small says he "purposely avoided direct mention" of its second theorem (That "... [T]he intellect proper ... constitutes the directive element of society, and only means by which the social forces can be controlled"),[14] because he is "in communcation with an increasing multitude of ministers and teachers who want to plunge into Sociology," now that he is at Chicago. For most this means "that they want references for a few months' reading to prepare themselves for the conquest of the world, but of the rabble a good many can be induced to begin at the bottom and build cautiously." Small re-assures his corresondent that he does not mean to dispute the second theorem, but these people "have only the most distant acquaintance with scientific method" and are "frightened by any unconventional suggestion." He then claims: "I can make some very cautious theologians study you with interest by telling them that I am far from being satisfied that you can justify all your conclusions, while I am satisfied that you have struck rock bottom with your method." Small thinks he can thus "accomplish more by vigorous dissent from some of" Ward's propositions, "than by unqualified acceptance." So Small becomes the devil's advocate; though he recalls again explicitly Ward's statement that he did not write "for the feeble minded."

Two letters written within a week of each other in the spring of 1895 complete this survey. In the first Small marks a further step in the progress of the discipline. One of the assistants to Archbishop Ireland of St. Paul,

Minnesota, had written to say that "he had been taking a class of young professional men (Catholics) through Small and Vincent's INTRODUCTION TO THE STUDY OF SOCIETY. The priest asked what to do next, and Small wrote that "the next thing to do was to take them through DYNAMIC SOCIOLOGY," which he did in spite of a caution from Small that the priest might be prevented from doing so "by the difference between his point of view and that of the author." Indeed, not only did the priest report that he was "using the book with his flock," but also that the Archbishop proposed to introduce Small and Vincent's text into the St. Paul seminary. "That thin edge of the wedge," Small observed, "may prepare the way for something more effective."

In the final letter Small speaks of Chamberlain's plans for the Institute and then turns to his own convictions:

"My personal belief is that Christ's life was the most effective object lession [sic] in history as to the **quality** of rational human life, but that it showed comparatively little about the **process.** Hence, no matter how extensive our resemblance to Christ in disposition, we are as little equipped thereby for social service as the raw recruit with loyalty alone is for war. Other things being equal, honest Christians ought to be the best social functionaries. Therefore I am glad to help get social knowledge in circulation among them, even if I do not hope to get much help from them in enlarging knowledge."

Elsewhere, too, Small remarked of his parents with great approbation that, "They took their religion seriously **as a high-minded manner of life.**"[15] What he admired was not what or who they believed but their practice of their convictions in an inner-worldly ethic. Small was convinced that a practical life based upon sociological **knowledge** could be achieved with a more perfect social union as a result:

"When we get a view of the world such as is commanded

from the sociological outlook, it turns out to be the theater of a plan of salvation more sublime than the imagination of religious creed-maker ever conceived. The potencies which God has put in man are finding themselves in human experience. This is the drama of life."[16]

The picture that emerges from this correspondence is that Small saw Christianity in basically **functional** terms-- as something that could be **used** to effect **performances** to benefit humanity. Just as he could state at one point that "Marx was one of the few really great thinkers in the history of social science," but completely reject his system;[17] so he apparently found no contradiction in proclaiming that "Jesus was, after all, the profoundest economist," while at the same time claiming that Christ's life showed little about how people ought to go about ordering their lives.[18] Sociology fit into this picture as the most comprehensive modality for enabling the essential transition from belief to practice. Although just how this was to occur was something Small could never clearly specify, he also intended that in this process belief-systems would be empirically tested and verified. It was at this point that Small segued from **episteme** to **gnosis**. In spite of his dogged commitment to research, Small could not adopt the "methodological atheism" of later social science.[19]

By 1910, Small was able to articulate clearly his vision of the new faith in a book entitled THE MEANING OF SOCIAL SCIENCE. He wrote that social science can never "be a substitute for religion," but "it is getting plainer and plainer ... that social science ... is the only rational body for religion." He continues:

"... [R]eligions have been men's more or less conscious attempts to give finite life its infinite rating. Science can never be an enemy of religion ... [T]he more science we have the more we are awed and lured by the mystery beyond our ken ... **And this is the heart of religion. It is the investment of such values as we have along with**

the best labor within our power to make them productive.
In this view social science carried into the creative stage
is the only conceivable body in which religion can be
vital.
Theological religions have always been ungenuine because
they have made the mystical the key to the real. The
religion of social science will make the real the key
to the mystical. In all seriousness then, and with careful
weighing of my words, I can register my belief that **social
science is the holiest sacrament open to men.** It is the
holiest because it is the wholest career within the terms
of human life.
... I am able to foresee no other development for religion
than the progressive sloughing off of its ritualistic attach-
ments and corresponding enrichment of its realistic content."[20]

Although Dibble rightly points out that Small drew back
from such pretentious sentiments in later life, he did
so not because of any new estimate of the value of traditional Christian teachings, but because his vision of the
power of social science narrowed.[21] Small's inconsis-
tencies on many points notwithstanding, his movement
from the Comtean heights is rooted in an underlying
and consistent commitment to serving the "DEMAND
FOR OBJECTIVITY" out of which he claims the **science**
of sociology grew.[22] This becomes abundantly clear
in comments made during his review of the early years
of American sociology--words not too different from
those of Weber a few years later in "Science as a Vocation." Some sociologists, Small admits, "have been carried
away by the more or less cultivated instincts of the
preacher," but he warns that a sociologist who

"... goes to preaching it as his leading occupation is pretty
sure to diminish his usefulness for any division of scientific
research which may not be strictly and safely indicental
to a preacher's experience ...
Sermonizing does not make astronomy, nor botany, nor

35

child psychology, nor sociology; no more does it furnish a worthy program for the pursuit of either science. There is a type of sociology which starts where it hopes to end. That is, it virtually does what the conventional preacher does when he announces his text. If there is a scientific technique corresponding to the name sociology, and if there is a substance of knowledge ascertainable by use of the technique, the immediate business of the investigator in sociology is to apply that technique so that it will reveal knowledge.

...[I]f as teachers we 'feature' the preaching value of sociology ... we virtually offer an emotional bribe for attention to a dubious subject. It would be an anticlimax after that to let our treatment drop down to the level of plain objective analysis."

This does not mean, however, that sociology is not a science capable of **practical application**, for Small continues:

"I should have no use for sociology if I did not believe that it is an essential factor in that veracious social science which must furnish the content of positive ethical theory. It is necessary to understand primary arithmetic in order to be able to understand what it means to be honest with our neighbor. It does not follow that the best way to learn arithmetic is to listen to sermons on the virtue of honesty. So with sociology and ethics."[23]

Small's retreat from sociological evangelism is not conditioned at all by religious convictions but by methodological concerns. He and Ward thus converge in both their opposition to Marxism and their aChristian commitment to science as the highest (i.e., most reliable) source of truth.

36

V

SOCIOLOGY AND THE SOCIAL GOSPEL

A number of the ideologues of the Social Gospel movement sometimes liked to call themselves "sociologists." "Practical Christianity," "Applied Christianity," and "Christian Sociology" each seemed to have a way of sliding into the other. This makes differentiating between sociology and the Social Gospel movement a sometimes tricky business. One can say that they were "often indistinguishable," as Morgan does for example, if one also recognizes that "often" does not mean "always," and that the Social Gospel movement itself was at least as multifaceted as early sociology.[1] Clearly the two movements had affinities and occasional interpenetrations, and they grew out of the same intellectual soil. But they can be distinguished from each other just as sociology and socialism can. The failed Institutes of Christian Sociology provide an important key here as well; for if the American Institute fell primarily over the sociology-socialism distinction, the Oberlin Institute set the Social Gospel apart from sociology. Admittedly making such distinctions always involves definitions: I can call myself a socialist, for example, but if I own a good-sized interest in General Motors, vote Republican, and attend the Southern Baptist church, the first designation is likely to strain the credulity of most observers. What we want to consider here is something of the process by which this "if-A-not-B" reaction developed in both sociology and religion.

Neither Small nor Ward confuses the two orientations, but Small does provide the critical and perplexing link between the two approaches. Despite his repudiation of historic Christianity, dogma, legalistic morality, and ecclesiastical hierarchy, Small had an affection for a Christ-concept throughout his life, as well as an abiding interest in man's "religious nature" (a quest for the infinite and an altruistic ethic). He wanted to use sociology

37

to educate the world, if it might be, into Christ-likeness, which for him simply meant respect for the worth of every human being. Sociology, then, would ultimately (and paradoxically) lead away from Christianity to Christ, from God to man. But sociology was the starting point. **Knowledge** of the social life of humanity was to exist **prior to** action. Small's plan began neither in the church nor on the streets but in the academy. He thus stood apart from both mainline Protestantism and the newer activistic stream of the Social Gospel, but he thought that each could be harnessed to implement his dream.

Nowhere is Small's "theology" more clearly in evidence than in his contribution to the "Christianity and the Modern World" lecture series at Chicago, entitled "Christianity and Industry."[2] Here Small seeks to define specifically what it is to be Christian. He quickly rejects all historic definitions and futher admits that in any collection of people there will be little agreement on what Christianity is or is not. The only accurate conclusion, he urges, is that Christianity is "whatever it was that Jesus taught," even though no one may now be able to decide for anyone else what that was. "It, not anyone's subsequent version of it, was Christianity." Thus, "... Christianity is thinking as Jesus thought about life, and feeling as Jesus felt about life, and willing as Jesus willed about life"; and "the indicated function of Christianity is to promote the Christian spirit." Christianity reduces by this method to solipsism. Its canon is entirely individuated and subjective. The very approach in Christian Sociology that Small despised he embraced when it came to theology. To be a Christian, for Small, is to share his humanism, which is at bottom a scientific humanism--a specific kind of respect for other human beings.

Again, he wrote in his will: "The longer I have studied human experiences the more convinced I have become that people can live together with satisfactory and reciprocal advantages only in the degree in which they learn to maintain a consistent Christian attitude toward one another ..."[3] Acknowledging even at the last an esteem for something in humanity essentially Christ-like, Small offers nothing in the way of a theological confession that would affirm the activity of God in the world today. That this kind of confession was shared by both traditionalists and the bulk of those actively involved in the Social Gospel movement is as much as anything else a line of demarcation between them on the one hand and sociology on the other.

By defining Christianity as he did, Small was at one and the same time able to retain "Christian Sociology" and rule out those who did not share his views. He could publish his own essay in the AMERICAN JOURNAL OF SOCIOLOGY, for example, and solicit or accept articles from any number of Social Gospel advocates--including both Josiah Strong and Walter Rauschenbusch, to whom Ahlstrom refers respectively as the "dynamo" and "passion and soul" of the movement--without necessarily aligning himself with them or abandoning his own convictions.[4] Small could get away with this, furthermore, because he was **editor** of the journal. Until fairly recently, being an editor of a journal, even in academe, meant that one published what she or he wanted to--to a large extent one's own work or that which agreed in fundamental principles with one's basic ideological commitments. Small was certainly not alone in this practice. It was engaged in by almost all the European Fathers and is to some extent being explicitly revived in sociology today. People who disagreed could write to the editor, of course, but they were more likely--particularly if their disagreements were systematic, rather than in details--to found another journal and enter the marketplace of ideas on their own. Small was thus the most critical figure in the development of American sociology, not only for his chairmanship of the Chicago department, but more significantly for his editorship of the A.J.S., which he controlled for thirty years, for twenty years was the only professional journal unique to the discipline in America, and preceded the founding of the American Sociological Society (largely also at Small's hands) by a decade.[5] To a great extent what was "genuine" sociology from 1895 to 1925 was that upon which Small placed his **imprimatur.**[6]

But Small also published his piece and others in the Social Gospel genre for irenic purposes. He desparately wanted to win the social gospellers to his side. He wanted them to believe that his sociology was Sociology, and thus **the** right basis for action. To do that he seems to have been willing to turn over some pages of issues to their direct interests--particularly in the face of his own admission that it was difficult to fill the pages of the infant journal with any material at all.[7] Small's occasional inclinations to piety in the A.J.S., however, must be balanced by his comments to Ward in their personal correspondence. ·He was trying to be all things to all people, that he might by all means win some. For reasons that are not entirely clear, Small considered it particularly important to reach those in the churches--perhaps to counter the "sociology" they had already been delivered, perhaps that his hegemony might be the more complete, perhaps because he felt the churches were a uniquely fertile soil for the planting of sociological seeds, perhaps a combination of the three. One can also not deny that the churches were bastions of middle-class respectability. Victory there could pay tremendous dividends in the wider institutional network, especially the colleges.

Ward and Small were not unique in their sociological faith. E.A. Ross and Charles A. Ellwood provide a similar couplet. Ross' SIN AND SOCIETY (1907), though "religous" in tone, is much more an indictment of traditional Christian morality than a reflection on the concept of "sin." Ross' solutions in that book, furthermore, are not in the Social Gospel vein, but are liberal-technocratic and political. One recent biographer, after a thorough analysis of Ross' religious views as expressed in his writings, concludes rather blandly that Ross "refused to reject the morality of his earlier beliefs, although he rejected their forms."[8] Indeed, in SOCIAL CONTROL Ross blasts one current of the Social Gospel movement explicitly when he complains that "The Christian cult of charity as a means of grace has formed a shelter under which idiots and cretins have crept and bred. The state gathers the deaf mutes into its sheltering arm, and a race of deaf mutes is in process of formation."[9] Yet he remained convinced of the commitment to applicability. When he was once asked to support a motion to limit membership in the Society to academicians and other "professionals," Ross replied: "Suckled in the practicalism of Lester F. Ward I wouldn't give a snap of my finger for the pussy-footing sociologist," whose "sneering at 'reformism' and condemning 'value judgments' ... suggest ... a rationalization or a ducking" of the issues.[10]

Though Ross claims in his autobiography that "dubious of what might follow on the crumbling of religion" he "kept silent" on religious matters "lo these forty-seven years," he was in fact hardly ever mum.[11] He spoke in his classes about the "myths" of the Old Testament and was a target of William Jennings Bryan's wrath in the 1920's.[12] In his early "Social Control" series for the A.J.S. (1896) he argues: "All-human, then, is the ultimate affirmation that is the corner stone of social religion. Not the doctrine about the gods, but the doctrine about men is the thing to be conserved."[13] Twenty-five years later, he still complains, "What an infinite pity that, at a time when pugnacity and greed have filled the world with woe ..., the churches should offer men the religion of obedience, propitiation, self-ingratiation, and safety, instead of the message of the fatherhood of God and the brotherhood of man."[14] Again, in his autobiography he reflects on his religious relations:

"For years I felt bitter towards the clergy for 'bulldozing' me. But after I found I could ignore the preachers and still hold a university chair I made a mute pact, 'You leave me alone and I'll leave you alone' ... I never assail

41

the cardinal Christian doctrines because, as interpreted by rare spirits, they are capable of affording great consolation and inspiring much good-will."[15]

Lacking Ross' frequent sarcasm, Ellwood is often contrasted with him on the matter of religiosity; yet both shared similar theological positions and the conviction that sociology was the only hope for Christianity. In THE RECONSTRUCTION OF RELIGION--a title instructive in itself--Ellwood argues that, "the religious revolution of the last two generations, which undermined theological Christianity ... has left the Church all but prostrate and powerless before the immense social task which now confronts it." Ignoring fundamentalism, which burgeoned during the same period, he claims that his book will "help show how the breath of life may again be breathed into its nostrils, and how the Church can again become that 'spiritual power' which the world needs to energize and harmonize its life." The breath of life that would provide "adequate motivation for a better social order" was not, however, an outpouring of the gifts of the Holy Spirit, but **social science**.[16] "Religion must enlist the scientific spirit and employ scientifically tested knowledge of human life if it is successfully to accomplish its task."[17] What we have had in the past "is not true Christianity, but rather theological and ecclesiastical systems ..., which have masqueraded as Christianity. What we need is to have the social implications of the Gospels widely and effectively taught."[18]

Very little of the Social Gospel material in the A.J.S. deviates from the Small-Ward-Ross-Ellwood style.[19] Over half of it is the work of one man, Shailer Mathews, who never claims to be a sociologist, but rather was a New Testament theologian who, like his old Colby classmate Small, had come to teach at the revived University of Chicago--eventually to be dean of its Divinity School. The bulk of Mathews' writing appears in a series of articles on "Christian Sociology" written for the initial journal issues of 1895-1896.[20] In the introductory piece,

Mathews admits the difficulty of the phrase and rejects definitions that emphasize either "the method by which results are obtained" or "the formation of such results." He wishes to take a more limited approach: "Christian sociology should mean the **sociology of Christ**; that is, the social philosophy and teachings of Christ. In this restricted sense the term is both legitimate and capable of an at least tentatively scientific content."[21] Mathews thus calls for a biblical exegesis that will generate scientific hypotheses that may be tested in order to separate religious truth from dogmatic falsehood.

A plausible explanation for Mathews' articles lies in his relationship to Small, and in turn Small's peculiar view of Christian Sociology and his position as editor of the A.J.S. Anxious to fill the pages of his new journal and bent on wooing churchmen to his view of sociology, Small asked his old friend--clearly an academic theologian--to help him out. Mathews would provide proof texts for Christian concern over social questions, while redefining "Christian Sociology" in a way more acceptable to Small's academic orientation of scientific humanism. Mathews was well-suited to the task because of his theological credentials on the one hand, and his faith in science as the arbiter of truth on the other. In his autobiography he writes approvingly of what his career effected:

"The substitution of the teachings of Jesus for authoritative doctrines ... the softening of God's sovereignty into a divine paternity, the development of the social gospel and the substitution of Christian nurture for supernatural conversion of children suffering from a corrupt human nature ..., [and] the modification of doctrines of the atonement were the direct result of the substitution of a scientific attitude for that of implicit reliance on the Bible demanded by orthodoxy."[22]

Like Small, Mathews' position stood apart from both radical

Christian socialism and fundamentalism. Both men were heirs of the **via media** adopted by Ely after his short flirtation with the radical wing, and all three placed investigation before action, without rejecting the conviction that their task was to make the world a better place to live.[23]

In 1895, too, Charles Henderson, Small's first colleague at Chicago--also appointed by Harper, considered by Small and all later authorities to be the more melioristically-oriented member of that department, and the only one of that period at Chicago not subsequently elected a president of the American Sociological Society--wrote a short editorial for the new A.J.S. distinguishing sociology from theology:

"Incalculable moral energies are generated by the emotional enthusiasm of religious societies ... [T]hese currents and torrents of religious feeling have great need of the precise methods, the painstaking knowledge of details, the exact measurement of available power, the clairvoyant common sense of the scientific mind ... Sociology, even in its present initial stage, is the most immediately useful scientific instrument for the teacher of ethics and religion. The sociological method is already beginning to revolutionize the mode of thinking in theology, in exegesis, in church history, in ethics and in pulpit rhetoric."[24]

Sociology, then, is not proceeding from the Social Gospel movement in Henderson's view. It is structuring it, perhaps even "redeeming" it.

Louis O. Wallis wrote a series of articles on "Biblical Sociology" for the journal from 1908 to 1911. These combine and explicate both Mathews' and Henderson's arguments. Wallis, who was neither an academician nor a clergyman but a professional writer and lecturer, came to attention in the A.J.S. first with the publication of an article, "The Capitalization of Social Development," in 1903 that had no religious content or reference. His name appears again when Small himself chose to review Wallis' book EGOISM: A STUDY IN THE SOCIAL PREMISES OF RELIGION in 1905. The editor writes that this is a significant book which attempts a "psycho-genetic" account of the religion of Israel: "The argument is specifically a thesis as to the precise reaction of interests which accounts for the history of Israel."[25] By 1907 Wallis wrote specifically for Small an article entitled "The Sociological Significance of the Bible." His emphasis here is on the necessity for "scientific treatment" of the Bible, which is "a fact for sociology before it is a fact for theological discipline. In other words, ... the Bible is primarily material for scientific treatment." The piece is an exposition of the nature and methods of Biblical higher criticism and a plea for sociologists to become involved in this **scientific** effort:

"Bible religion is an involution of the common ethical struggle, conditioned by the special circumstances of Bible history. Its conceptions and institutions are the result of a development which passes through a number of crises, each disclosing a composition of **interests**-- priestly and prophetic, conservative and radical, rural and urban. It is the merit of the literary stage of biblical criticism to show us the nature of the documents. It is the merit of the historical stage to emphasize the fact of development. It will be the merit of the sociological stage to indicate how this development took place."[26]

Later in the same year, Wallis wrote a follow-up article, "Sociology and Theism." Here he claims that in addition to his argument in the earlier paper that "higher criticism of the Bible must be made in the light of sociology before its work is completed," he will show that "sociological criticism delivers the biblical material over to theism in better form than do preceding stages of inquiry into the Bible."[27] Thus the substance of his argument is for a **readjustment** of theology based on sociological inqiry. The action-evangelism of the social gospel is nowhere in evidence; though there is a consciousness of the effects of social structures (e.g., class struggle) upon historical development--an important premise of scientific and academic sociology. The "Biblical Sociology" essays explicate these themes and were subsequently published in book form as well by the University of Chicago Press. These papers were academic, at least quasi-scientific, scholarly attempts at serious Biblical criticism and likewise bespoke nothing of the reform spirit that characterized the Social Gospel movement.

By contrast, however, an article written by Rauschenbusch in 1896 virtually sparkles with the rhetoric of the work of the Holy Spirit, the soldiers of the Lamb, the Cross and the Crown. **But** more important than the article to an understanding of its relationship to the development of sociology is the fact that Small added a rare disclaiming editorial footnote to the title: "The author is corresponding secretary of 'the Brotherhood of the Kingdom', and this paper is written from the point of view of that organization." Thus Small--the discipline's official censor--draws a line of separation between this manifestation of the Social Gospel movement and social science. Rauschenbusch does write again in 1897 without a disclaimer, but also without the language of a faith commitment. Here in a much more pragmatic vein he claims the work "is not an appeal to conscience, but to the more delicately developed faculty of looking out for our own interest." There is no attempt to identify sociology with the Social Gospel in these pieces, much less render the two "indistinguishable." Instead there is the genteel Machiavellianism that **is** an ineluctable characteristic of Small's management strategy for sociological self-definition.[28]

During this same period, for example, Small himself published two essays on the matter of what sociology is and where it fits into related developments. Titled "The Sociologists' Point of View" and "The Meaning of the Social Movement," both **distinguish** between the sociologist and the humanitarian reformer generally.

In line with Small's applied emphasis, however, neither discounts the value of social action. The grammar of the title of the former article may represent a printer's error, but it is more likely to represent an effort by Small to speak **ex cathedra** for sociology as a whole. The tendency to publish religious pieces was not restricted to the A.J.S. They also appeared in SOCIAL FORCES, though these were "of a far more pedestrian nature."[29] This does not, however, entail the conclusion that there was an alliance between sociology and Christianity--any more than does the publication of Paul Tillich's "Protestantism in the Present World Situation" in the A.J.S. in 1938. Small's relations with many of the prominent Social Gospel leaders can also be traced through his reviews of their works.

Another representative article by E.M. Fairchild, a Social Gospel leader, completes this survey.[30] He says, in part:

"The rise of sociology is the salvation of the church, because by the application of the sociologic method the function of the church as a social institution can be accurately defined. The church has all along been of service, though indirectly and by somewhat crude methods, in the struggle for self-realization ... The church is, therefore, in the last analysis, an educational institution."

The final line summarizes most succinctly the relationship between Small and the Social Gospel movement. Knowledge was the core of Small's faith. If it could be deomonstrated that the primary function of the church was to convey knowledge, then it could become an arm of the academy. Though differing slightly in his approach, Ross took the same general viewpoint in an 1897 article simply titled "The Educational Function of the Church." Lacking an anti-clericalism such as that which developed in France, the church in America would be the agent of scientific "moral education" in this country that only the school could be for Durkheim.[31] Small and Durkheim thus shared a common sociological faith but were part of different cultures. The Social Gospel movement was important to early American sociology because it focused attention upon social problems. As it did so, it provided an entry for sociological knowledge into an apparent theological void.

VI

RECONSTRUCTING THE SOCIOLOGICAL PAST IN AMERICA

The purpose of this essay has been to argue that far too much has been made of the religiosity of early American sociologists. To a man they were practically all secular humanists, whose Protestant sentiments were more a reflection of their cultural time and space than of any faith in the historic Christian revelation. So far, we have looked primarily at the works of the Fathers themselves. Several additional pieces of evidence may also be cited.

First, a series of articles by Harold Bolce that appeared in COSMOPOLITAN in 1909: with titles like "Blasting at the Rock of Ages" and "Polyglots in the Temple of Babylon," the series railed against the anti-supernaturalism of the Fathers and other academics. Giddings, for example, is reported to have said that America has specialized in religious lunacy, and Sumner is pictured as destroying the basis for an absolute God-given, unchanging morality. Edwin Earp, a former clergyman, professor at Syracuse and then at Drew, is said to have claimed it "unscientific" that "God ever turned stonemason and chiseled command-ments on a rock."[1] While these articles are clearly sarcastic and written with an axe to grind, they hardly suggest an affinity between sociology and popular concep-tions of religion.

Second, James Leuba's BELIEF IN GOD AND IMMORTAL-ITY published in 1916, showed that only twenty-nine

48

percent of the "lesser" sociologists and nineteen percent of the "greater" sociologists expressed belief in a personal God. Whereas these data were based upon questionnaire responses from a sample of American Sociological Society members (among others), such a report hardly confirms a positive relationship between Christian faith and early sociology in America. Although by no means all persons teaching sociology were members of the Society, the leaders, major writers, and opinion shapers were.[2]

Third, in addition to the Holbrook survey and Leuba's work, there were several other research projects less specifically focused on the religion question, but useful all the same. In 1894 Ira Howerath surveyed "all teachers of sociology" in the United States--though with no indication of how he located these persons. Forty replies were received, of which thirty-seven were useable. Three-quarters thought sociology a science, while practically none wanted it taught with ethics (the closest option to religion in the instrument).[3] Starting in 1902, Frank Tolman published a series of articles on the status of sociological instruction in the United States for the A.J.S. These reveal no particular religious bias in the courses of instruction, nor a clear emphasis on a specific program of reform.[4] In the late 1920's, L.L. Bernard realized that most of the early Fathers remained alive but were aging; so he decided to obtain life histories of as many as possible using a relatively systematic outline format. Slightly over 250 responses were received. No specific questions on religion were included, but the subjects were asked to discuss their backgrounds and people and experiences leading to their decisions to become sociologists and their formation of sociological worldviews. Over half made some reference to religious affiliation, but only a third treated it in detail. Among these, furthermore, the focus of the discussion went in several directions: some came to sociology because of positive religious experiences, some out of negative reactions, and some simply mentioned it without making an explicit

49

connection between the two areas.[5] While a relatively large percentage had fathers who were ministers, furthermore, this number is not very different from that noted in Veysey's study of the backgrounds of over a hundred prominent professors of all subjects who taught at American universities during the last three decades of the nineteenth century.[6] Ministerial parentage is probably more of a commentary on the character of American higher education in the late nineteenth century than the content of any particular discipline. Perhaps one could even spin some secularization theory out of it, but not in itself an explanation of the character of sociological theory in America.

Finally, if we look at the sociology that was being produced during these formative years, it is not hard to see that an enormous amount of writing was being done without any noticeable reference to religious questions. In the very critical years for Christian Sociology of 1894 and 1895, for example, an intense debate took place in the pages of the ANNALS on the nature of sociology. The parties included Small, Ward, Giddings, and Simon Patten, each of whom had addressed religious questions or audiences; yet the debate was entirely secular, without religious overtone or inuendo.[7] Ely and Commons made and maintained their reputations on secular issues and substantive treatises. A paradoxical confusion about how to go on in modernity and a zeal for a better world pervaded all disciplines and walks of life in this period. It affected sociology because sociology as much as any other form of knowledge is a part of a particular time and place, but it did not determine its form or content in a way different from other intellectual pursuits.

Although it is thus true that there were a number of men in early American sociology who were ministers or who had theological training--some of whom may well have been desperate men--those who fully embraced the profession apparently did so as an alternative to the historic Christian tradition at least as often as accepting it. They had a new gospel to proclaim, and any interest they showed in the church was merely an extension of their academic commitments. Scientific knowledge was the source of the world's redemption, not a crucified and risen Lord.

There is no doubt that Protestant values informed the culture of the early American Fathers. As reflective people with a history, they were keenly aware of this fact. To focus on the religious interests of the Fathers, however, is to miss the point. Their formative influences lay not in historic Christianity but in the spirit of the times. These in turn belong more properly to the sociology of science than the sociology of religion. Every scientist, as a result of common human being, is influenced by upbringing and socio-cultural worldview. It is the contention of at least one branch of social science, however, that these potential biases can be known and controlled in research and analysis. If we are concerned about early American sociology, it is measures of these kinds of things that should now be uppermost in our investigations. Early American sociology should be judged not by its origins but by its contributions to the understanding and prediction of human behavior. Rare indeed, one suspects, are the chemists whose research and theory are analyzed in the context of whether they or their fathers were ministers.

But what of the original questions of what happened in the course of the development of American sociology to create a situation in which only symbolic interactionism of the myriad schools of sociological thought today is willing to trace its ancestry from American sources, and why the European thinkers have come to be the major figures of the discipline, while the work of the Americans is largely glossed? We have thus far investigated some aspects of the early development of sociology in America primarily as a way of setting the stage for some possible answers to these questions--particularly those that revolve around the supposed religious interests of the early American Fathers. We can now assess how well various explanations that have been offered serve to order the data.

One of the simplest and most ubiquitous reasons given for the fall of most of the early Fathers from disciplinary grace is that they were preacher-types who had little appreciation for sociology as a scientific discipline. May this essay demolish such a concept once and for all. Although their methodological techniques were certainly unsophisticated and their theories often unsubstantiated by evidence or even illogical, these men were clearly and thoroughly committed to **science** as a vocation and to sociology as a science. It was patently naive to assume because a man's father was a minister or he himself took course work at a seminary or even was ordained that his sociology was a positive and integrated outgrowth of Christian faith and as such unscientific. It is just as tenable a hypothesis--if not more so--to think that such men went to sociology to break with what they found to be an **inefficient** means to accomplish the goals they felt were necessary either for sociology or themselves (or both). We can equally well conclude that these men saw in sociology as science a hope for "redeeming" American society that they had not seen in denominational Chrisitianity--or even the Social Gospel. There is no justification in the substantive data of the period to support the analytical posture that a theological background or education would necessarily lead to a more-or-less orthodox Christianity, or that early American sociology was but a means for bringing that particular theological stance "warmed over" into a stronger intellectual position. Sociology was an alternative to both the Social Gospel and Christian Socialism. It was the substitution of explanatory propositions in the language of science for the language of religion or politics. Thus Small writes:

" ... [The] sociologists presented a clear case of coping with a condition, whatever role was played before, at the time, or afterward by their own or other people's theories. This condition was that [of] the squatter sovereignty exercised by earlier comers in the social science field ... [T]o get a hearing the sociologists had to meet the conditions which they encountered, in the only way that was open to them in the then existing state of mind about the relation of subject matter to academic departments. They had to appear in the name of a 'science' in order to get standing in court."[8]

Mainline Protestantism was perceived as incapable of responding adequately to the crises of urbanization and industrialization that were concurrent with the upheaval of the intellectual stratum in the wake of scientific research during the nineteenth century. Sociology developed as an attempt to provide an empirically grounded comprehensive system of **knowledge** upon which to build the good society. Fearful of Marxism and discouraged by Christianity, the Fathers looked to a scientific "technology" to provide a human and humane solution to life's problems.

This, however, leads to a second hypothesis for the decline of early American sociology. Shaskolsky states the matter most succinctly when he says that the Americans were concerned with "social problems," while the Europeans addressed "the social problem."[9] On the surface, this juxtaposition seems to have a ring of truth, but if probed but a little, its weaknesses become quickly apparent. As the Schwendingers point out in at times painful detail, the problem of order, of change and control, lay at the bottom of the work of almost all of the early American Fathers, and is addressed explicitly by Sumner, Ward, Small, Weatherly, Ross, and the work of Park and Burgess. Furthermore, only the most cursory reading of Durkheim, Weber, or Marx would lead one to think that they were unconcerned about "social problems." If anything, indeed, Shaskolsky's premise is evidence for the extent to which the contemporary interests of American sociology have reinterpeted the European Fathers in order to ignore their reform impetus.[10]

A third hypothesis, with a good deal more credibility as far as it goes, is that American sociology in the early years is not to be credited as good scientific work because of its **reform** impetus. But this must be abandoned as well, for it too is based on half-truths. Yes, the Americans were reform oriented, but **so were the Europeans.** That Marx was concerned about changing the world is readily obvious. Durkheim's overriding concern, however, was also reformist--**moral education** and the fostering of the good society in France. Likewise, Weber's relationship to politics and especially the concept of the **wertfrei** sociologists have been so miscontrued by American sociology as to have almost completely obscured the reformist ideals that underlay his work. On the other hand, Marx, Weber, and Durkheim--none mainline Christians--all studied religion as a major variable in their work, and all considered themselves to be scientists.[11] While each operated very differently and had divergent ideas about the content, methods, scope, and results of sociology, they nevertheless **shared** with the Americans similarities of focus and discipline.

As a more adequate explanation, we can start by recognizing that the dominant forms of sociological thought in America have from the beginning to the present been essentially Comtean in character. This may not be true for radical Marxism or certain versions of symbolic interactionism, but in the main it is clear. It has come down to us through Ward, Durkheim, and Parsons as well as a host of other figures, even though in an increasingly secular society its vocabulary has become proportionately more sophisticated. That Friedrichs in 1970 found the terms "prophetic" and "priestly" more apt metaphors than any others to discuss sociology's developmental wanderings is of no little significance. Throughout its history sociology has been characterized by a religious non-theism--an agnosticism toward the **theos,** but a religion of quasi-empirical **gnosis.**[12]

Secondly, sciology has always been dominated by **functionalism** in some form or other. Perrin has pointed out the extent to which Spencer's functionalism has been slighted by many students of social theory.[13] Sumner, Ward, Small, Ross, Weatherly, and a covey of other early figures were all functionalists. In addition, a large number--though certainly not all--of the Amerian Fathers had studied in Germany, even if they actually took their doctorates here. Others, by studying under their direct tutilage when they returned, were "informed" by the German tradition. Thus, while sociology bloomed in its fullest flower in America, it looked to continental thinkers--French and German--for its inspiration from the beginning.

What blurred this sighting was World War I and on its heels the Marxist-Leninist revolution in Russia. The War produced extreme anti-German feelings in the United States. People with German names changed them, and things associated with Germany were proscribed. Contact between the scholarly communities in the two nations reached a nadir. American sociology was left very much on its own and in some cases on the defensive about its heritage. The Russian revolution and the subsequent "Red Scare" added the compounded problem that anything even remotely connected with "socialism" was suspect. To this academic sociology responded by consolidating to emphasize its Americanism and **de**emphasize the reform impetus that might connect it to socialism. Sociology seemed bent on proving more than anything else that it was science in service to country. Thus it focused on smaller problems and eschewed any schemes that might be interpreted as questioning the basic forms of American social organization. This orientation found its highest expression in the grand theory of the Chicago School under Park and Burgess. The Great Depression created financial conditions that hardly promoted cross-Atlantic graduate study for many Americans, and concurrently provided manifold theses topics at home.[14]

55

Onto this scene came the young Talcott Parsons and THE STRUCTURE OF SOCIAL ACTION in 1937.[15] The book provided a voluntaristic functionalist integration of four leading European thinkers' works into a systems paradigm and revolutionized thinking in academic sociology--particularly after the intermezzo of World War II. Later, of course, a revolution itself began against Parsons, and part of that revolution was a searching of the "scriptures" upon which the "faith" was founded. But--and this may be the most lasting testimonial to Parsons--when the scriptures began to be searched, they were those that underlay **Parsons'** version of the proper **gnosis**. Except for the reawakening of interest in Marx-- but Marx was one of the figures upon whom Parsons wrote his doctoral dissertation at Heidelberg--it was Parsons who gave us Durkheim and Weber.[16] Here, I suggest, is the explanation of why we turn to the Europeans and which Europeans it is to whom we turn. Whether or not we continue to accept Parsons' theories, we are still operating in reference to the disciplinary framework that he defined, and this was one that virtually excluded American social thought prior to his own time."[17]

NOTES

I

ON THE CONSTRUCTION OF A
SOCIOLOGICAL PAST IN AMERICA

1. Although many early sociologists were advocates of women's rights and universal suffrage--Ward being foremost--the fact remains that the discipline, like practically all others at the time, was male dominated. The use of male terminology is thus historically appropriate when referring to the leadership of the profession in its formative years.

2. See Swatos, 1980. That this **is** a problem for the sociology of science can be seen from Gerver's comment twenty years ago introducing his book on Ward: "... Comte, Ward, and to a lesser extent, Marx, are also regarded as unworthy of more than antiquarian interest" (1963: 2-3). I show Marx to be the most cited theorist in contemporary texts, but Gerver is correct for 1963.

3. Hinkle's FOUNDING THEORY OF AMERICAN SOCIOLOGY (1980) and Bierstedt's AMERICAN SOCIOLOGY (1981) are notable exceptions, but as such prove the rule.

4. This is not to say that symbolic interactionism has no European roots. It may be traced in the writings of the Scottish moralists, for example. The point, however, is that current interactionists do not feel obliged to cite European forebears for their work, or appear embarrassed by American Fathers.

5. Morgan, 1969: 42; Schwendinger & Schwendinger, 1974; Hinkle & Hinkle, 1954; Oberschall, 1972. Also

Carey, 1975; Fine, 1979; Fuhrman, 1978, 1980; Fukuyama, 1963; Hadden et al., 1974; Janowitz, 1972; Lazarsfeld, 1962; Mills, 1943; Reed, 1981; Westby, 1978; Williams, 1976; and Wolff, 1946.

6. See Bernard & Bernard, 1943; Fine, 1979; Fuhrman, 1980; Hinkle, 1980; Oberschall, 1972; O'Connor, 1942; and Schwendinger & Schwendinger, 1974.

7. The Bernards write of Comte: "As heart and center of his remedial program he had proposed a new religious system which should be built upon the principles of science--the sciences of human nature and of social organization ... He, too, like the theologians themselves, believed strongly in the importance of religion ... Like them, he believed that one must reach most men through the human heart, that is, through the emotions ... But unlike them, he knew that the framework of such an emotional religion can be so built that it will possess validity and social usefulness only if it is constructed according to the blueprints of science" (1943: 217).

8. So Rosenberg (1963: 4): "From the Founding Fathers of the Republic to the founding fathers of sociology there is a straight line of compulsive hope."

9. Hinkle writes: "... [H]umanitarianism tends to evoke efforts at reform either from a more religious or more secular basis. If they issue from a more secular foundation, they tend to presuppose or at least to be associated with the doctrine of progress. And ... progress ... tends to involve the welfare of increasingly broader aggregates of persons up to mankind as a whole. In its older religious form, humanitarianism conceives of the Christian brother-hood of all mankind ... with the unavoidable implication that each person is indeed his brother's keeper" (1980: 32). That sociology's evolutionism was not merely reactive is confirmed by Martindale's note (1960: 66, n. 18) that "Darwin, in THE ORIGIN OF SPECIES (1859), mentioned Spencer as one of his predecessors"; also see Fine, 1979.

10. See Shils, 1948.

11. Young, 1896: 370-371.

12. See Jones, 1968; Dressner, 1972.

13. See Voegelin, 1952. I am indebted to Toby Huff for suggesting the importance of the distinction between **episteme** and **gnosis.** I think both were operating in early American sociology, whereas he opts for only the former; see Dynes, 1974.

14. For a cross-cultural example, see Arjomand, 1982.

15. I thus treat Christianity in something like what Barker calls "the reportive rather than the stipulative sense" (1981: 262). In traditional terms, this is much closer to a real than a nominal definition, though I am not entirely comfortable with that phrasing of the distinction. I would certainly not deny that it is possible to make "Jesus" into almost anyone/thing conceptually that one wants--and Marx, too, for that matter--nor that something of this sort has not occurred in every generation. To substitute this esoteric concept in an analytical work for that held by the large body of devotees, however, only deepens the quagmire (see Vree, 1976).

16. See, e.g., Poloma, 1982; Cavanaugh, 1982.

17. See Page, 1940.

18. Berger, 1963: 23.

II

IN THE BEGINNING, SUMNER

1. Small, 1916: 732; see McCloskey, 1951: 34-39.

2. In Curtis, 1981: 13.

3. See Curtis, 1981: Starr, 1925. Of Sumner's subsequent relations with the Church, Curtis reports that he officiated at a grandson's baptism, ushered at New Haven's Trinity Church, and "reportedly" received the Holy Communion shortly before his last illness (1981: 42).

4. In Starr, 1925: 543.

5. So Curtis, 1981: 62. Sumner had tried to use his training in biblical criticism at Trinity upon his return from Europe. He learned: "I speedily found that there was no demand at all for 'biblical science'; that everybody was afraid of it, especially if it came with the German label on it. It was a case in which, if a man should work very hard and achieve remarkable results, the only consequence would be that he would ruin himself." Eventually he went to New York to work on a new journal called LIVING CHURCH (not THE LIVING CHURCH), "which several 'broad' Episcopal clergyman had established to 'find harmony between Revelation and science ... meet the practical and social problems of Christianity at this day, and prove the reality of the Kingdom of God in its work'." The journal lasted only a year; then Sumner left for full-time pastoral work in Morristown, New Jersey.

6. Youmans & Youmans, 1880.

7. It is a current convention in the history of sociology to dissociate Sumner from humanistic sociology, but that overstates the case. Sumner was a humanist, but his humanism was essentially different from that of Ward, Small, and the subsequent mainstream of American sociology.

8. Sumner, 1910: 591. Immediately following this essay is one by Ellwood which completely anticipates Homans' psychological reductionism.

III

INSTITUTES OF CHRISTIAN SOCIOLOGY

1. Rader, 1966: 64. Rader adds that in his autobiography, Ely recalls his association with Chautauqua as beginning in 1884 at the invitation of Bishop Vincent, but actual correspondence in the Ely MSS confirms the 1887 date and Harper's agency.

2. Rader, 1966: 60-61.

3. Ely, 1889: 9.

4. In Rader, 1966: 64. How accurate this assessment is may reflect Small's interests as much as the facts. As we will see, Stuckenberg claims credit for introducing the term, and Graham Taylor held the first chair of Christian Sociology. Coincidentally, Stuckenberg subsequently wrote introductory texts that competed with Small's, while Taylor's Department of Christian Sociology was just down the street from Small's Chicago department.

5. Smith (1970) erroneously refers to this group as the "American Society for Christian Sociology," and gives a rather misleading account of its character and importance. Even worse is the careless account provided by Dombrowski (1936), who hopelessly intermingles the American and Oberlin institutes. Lyon (1983) largely picks up on Dombrowski and further muddies the waters. Stern's account in the Small-Ward correspondence (1933) has less problems, but is still weak on details. I have tried to make sense out of this movement from what records remain and believe that the current account is the only accurate one.

6. ANNALS, 1893.

7. Commons, 1934: 51.

8. ANNALS, 1893; Crafts, 1907: 240.

9. A variety of "membership lists" for the American Institute appear in the Ely MSS; see Furner, 1975. The work and career of Graham Taylor provide a valuable contrast against which to set the subsequent development of American sociology. He was one of the few people to take Christian Sociology seriously on its own terms and stick with it. He also disappeared very quickly from the sociological mainstream. In his autobiography he never mentions the Institute of Herron, and Ely only peripherally; though his biographer corrects these omissions. See Taylor, 1930: esp. pp. 378-406, Wade, 1964.

10. In Rader, 1966: 134-135, also see Furner, 1975: 151.

11. It is difficult to assess the significance of autobiographical omissions--or inclusions, for that matter. One possible measure of the contemporary significance of the Institute (on the negative side) is that the July and August issues of the New York TIMES carried considerable material on both the Chautauqua meetings and Ely's Wisconsin trial. In neither context--or anywhere else--is the Institute mentioned. With the exception of the materials cited here, this is also true of other popular periodicals of the day.

12. See Rader, 1966; Furner, 1975.

13. See Rader, 1966: 151.

14. Commons, 1934: 51. Here Commons gives a single sentence summary of the Institute's aims: "...[T]o present Christ as the living Master and King and Christian law as the ultimate rule for human society, to be realized on earth." Summaries of the Grinnell addresses may be found in SCARLET AND BLACK, 1894; HERALD, 1894a,b,c. See Taylor (1930: 24-26) for a valuable account of the role of women in organizing the Columbia Exposition

sessions.

15. Stern, 1933: 171; nevertheless Herron had well-known Debs sympathies.

16. REVIEW, 1894: 749.

17. See Barnard, 1969: 94; Mott, 1938(I): 739-724. In his autobiography, Wright writes: "... Z. Swift Holbrook, at once an enterprising businessman, a sound theologian, and an ardent promoter of sensible views of Christian sociology, joined me in the purchase of the magazine from Mr. E.J. Goodrich, the former Oberlin publisher. Mr. Holbrook's busines ability gave a new impetus to the publication, which it has felt ever since" (1916: 395). Holbrook may well have had his interest in BIBLIOTHECA SACRA stimulated by the acquisition of control over the NORTHWESTERN CONGREGATIONALIST by Herron, who turned it into KINGDOM, a journal to advance his point of view. Herron's resignation from Grinnell and Holbrook's death occurred within a year of each other; thus largely ending the journalistic war. The critical point of contention for the two seems to have been Herron's support of Eugene B. Debs and Holbrook's opposition to him. Holbrook frequently has very nice things to say about Herron as a human being.

18. Barnard, 1969: 84-97, 149.

19. Barnard, 1969: 95-96; also see Baker, 1973.

20. Crafts, 1907: 421 (originally published 1895).

21. Holbrook, 1895a; also see 1894, 1896. All of the ensuing quotations are from the 1895 survey, where they appear in alphabetical order by the last name of the contributor. Additional definitions appear in Crafts, 1907: 239-40.

22. Holbrook, 1895b: 563.

23. Stuckenberg's subsequent works themselves betray the shift. In 1898 he published an INTRODUCTION TO THE STUDY OF SOCIOLOGY and in 1903 a two-volume SOCIOLOGY. By this time, no mention is made of Christian Sociology. Instead Stuckenberg takes pride in his introduction of a special division of the new discipline: sociological ethics. Many similar themes are advanced under this heading, but in clearly secular discourse. Also see Stuckenberg, 1885, 1893.

24. Holbrook, 1896: 172-173.

25. Small, 1895b.

26. This synopsis is drawn from Barnard, 1969; Commons, 1934; Dombrowsi, 1936; Ely, 1938; Furner, 1975; Harter, 1962; Rader, 1966; and Wright, 1916.

27. In Stern, 1933: 171.

28. ANNALS, 1895: 182-183.

29. In Stern, 1933: 172.

30. Small, 1895a: 15; see Lyon, 1983. Another important difference was that English Christian Sociology and Christian Socialism primarily grew out of the "High Church" wing of the Church of England and thus had a traditionalistic foundation. American Christian Sociology grew out of a piety that exulted in an abandonment of tradition. This is what made it so difficult for American Christian Sociologists to define what it was that made their sociology Christian.

31. Small wrote his "all the help I can" letter April 10, 1895. On April 25, at Harper's request, he sent a detailed proposal to the Chicago trustees inducing them to support a journal. There is no mention there of Christian Sociology; rather he writes: "I have been urged by some of the leaders of Sociological investigation in this country,

64

Lester F. Ward the Nestor of American Sociological investigation among the number, to take the editorship of such a journal" (Dibble, 1975: 163-168, reprints the entire letter; this quote is on p. 164).

32. In Holbrook, 1895a: 479.

33. Commons, 1934: 51.

34. Ely, 1894: 88-90.

35. In Rader, 1966: 151.

36. ANNALS, 1895: pp. 28-33.

37. OUTLOOK, 1893: 134-135. An explanation for this can only be conjectural. My own would be that Herron demanded the more radical version that was adopted at Chautauqua. Whether Ely or Vincent supplied the material to Abbott in advance, Ely obviously liked it, as did the Episcopalian bishops. On the OUTLOOK, see Mott, 1938(III): 422-435. Dombrowski, who obviously has axes to grind, places Abbott along with Shailer Mathews (see below) into the class of "hypocritical" leaders of the Social Gospel movement (versus true Christian Socialists); see 1936: 20-30.

38. Commons, 1934: 51-52. Herron was also inspired by Mazzini, at least in his early years. For a relatively contemporary account of this Italian Christian Socialist leader see MacCunn, 1907: 185-212.

IV

SMALL AND WARD

1. In Dealy, 1927: 75; see Chugerman, 1939; Scott, 1976.

2. Ward, 1895: 21-22.

3. Scott, 1976: 136.

4. Dealy, 1927: 65; Scott, 1976: 139; Stern, 1935.

5. Dealy, 1927: 65-67; Scott, 1976: 135-164; Chugerman, 1939: 1-10; Schwendinger & Schwendinger, 1974: 184-186.

6. Ward, 1895: 18; **pace** Merton and current sociology of science.

7. Although Ward scores Sumner for his biologism, he was equally biologistic, as Patten (of the University of Pennsylvania) was fond of noting. Small, in turn, accepted this biologism. See Ward, 1894; Patten, 1894a,b; Small, 1895c. On the Small and Vincent text's popularity, see Clow, 1920.

8. Christakes, 1978: 29-30; and Lazarsfeld, 1962: 758.

9. Neither Small nor Ward left an intentional autobiography. Small's "Fifty Years of Sociology in the United States" (1916) can be read as having autobiographical overtones. From Ward we have diary materials for the pre-sociology years (Stern, 1935) and some commentary accompanying the essays that form GLIMPSES OF THE COSMOS (1913-1918).

10. Dibble, 1975: 92. Dibble has the greatest amount of material on Small's religiosity; see e.g., pp. 60-62, 79-80, 239-240.

11. Small, 1890: 81. Harry Elmer Barnes, whose THE TWILIGHT OF CHRISTIANITY (1929) is probably one of the most anti-religious books ever written by a sociologist, writes positively of Small that he was ethical, not doctrinal or moralistic, and that "he powerfully promoted the movement to take" ethical questions "out of supernaturalism and metaphysics" (1926: 19,44).

12. Unless otherwise cited, all quoted correspondence comes from Stern, 1933.

13. Italics mine.

14. Ward, 1892: 5.

15. Goodspeed, 1926: 1.

16. In Dibble, 1975: 53 (originally written, 1906).

17. Small, 1912: 809; on Small and Marx, see Dibble, 1975: 129-133. Martindale (1960: 189-196) treats Small as a conflict theorist, but not a Marxist.

18. In Dombrowski, 1936: 9 (originally written 1890).

19. See Berger, 1969: 179-185, 199 n. 36.

20. Small, 1910: 275 (italics mine). By contrast, much contemporary sociology of religion finds ritual, mystical, and symbolic elements of religion essential to its social function.

21. Thus Dibble, 1975; see Becker, 1971.

22. Small, 1916; 748. Elsewhere he wrote: "The first commandment with promise for graduate schools is: Remember the research ideal, to keep it holy!" (in Dibble, 1975: 54). Also see his "Social Value of an Academic Career," reprinted in full in Dibble (pp. 185-200), which makes Small's priorities crystal clear and should still all murmerings about his "ministerial career."

23. Small, 1916: 852-854.

V

SOCIOLOGY AND THE SOCIAL GOSPEL

1. See Morgan, 1969; Hadden, et al., 1974; Reed, 1981; and though not without its problems, Dombrowski, 1936: 9-30.

2. Small, 1920; see Small, 1901.

3. In Goodspeed, 1926: 14.

4. Ahlstrom, 1972: 798-802.

5. The A.J.S. was not the first American sociology journal, but it was the first to endure and the first to treat sociology as a professional scientific discipline unto itself (see Davis & Perrin, 1982). Of course, sociologists had access to other professional academic journals, most notably the ANNALS, and it was the American Academy that published Giddings' THE THEORY OF SOCIOLOGY, which is something of an American masterwork, in 1893, as a special issue.

6. A number of Small's books (1905, 1907, 1909, 1924) also construct a history of sociology--or sociological antecedents. In these Small rules theorists in and out of consideration for the "proper" development of the discipline. These complement Small, 1916.

7. Thus Small, 1916: 786. Small can be a little more "up front" here largely because he has realized disciplinary hegemony.

8. Weinberg, 1972: 85.

9. Ross, 1901: 424.

10. Ross, 1936: 180. Bierstedt (1981: 492-493) is clearly

wrong when he argues that "the normative taboo" of value free social science was accepted by the Americans on their own as far back as Small and Ward. That value neutrality--or knowledge for its own sake--was accepted in some quarters, notably Columbia, is true, but it was not generalized and was a bone of contention into the 'twenties at least.

11. Ross, 1936: 119.

12. See White, 1952: 116.

13. Ross, 1896: 442.

14. Ross, 1920: 133-134.

15. Ross, 1936: 117-118.

16. Ellwood, 1922: ix; see 1913.

17. Ellwood, 1923: 9.

18. Ellwood, 1920: 132.

19. On Small and Ross, see Dibble, 1975: 58-64. This is also true for material in the other two journals that appeared within the period: SOCIAL FORCES and SOCIOLOGY AND SOCIAL RESEARCH (see Reed, 1975).

20. G.F. Wright was particularly perturbed by this series after Small's attitude toward Christian Sociology expressed in BIBLIOTHECA SACRA (see Wright, 1896: 378). Furner (1975: 151, n. 10) rightly terms Mathews' series "an example of the academic protest against Christian sociology." One of the many misunderstandings of early American sociology has come from not giving adequate attention to what Mathews acctually said through this series, which was not an encomium for Christian sociology.

21. Mathews, 1895: 69-70.

22. Mathews, 1936: 231; 1910.

23. By 1929, however, William Ogburn, a Columbia product, would address the Society as president to say that "sociology as a science is not interested in making the world a better place to live ... science is interested in only one thing, to wit, discovering new knowledge" (in Reed, 1982: 190). This is entirely antithetical to the Ward-Small orientation, both of whom held that science is interested in discovering new knowledge in order to make the world a better place to live. The separation to them would have been mindless.

24. Henderson, 1895: 383.

25. Small, 1906: 848-849.

26. Wallis, 1907a: 532, 551.

27. Wallis, 1907b: 838.

28. Rauschenbusch, 1896, 1897: 18, see 1907; also Singer, 1926.

29. Reed, 1981: 40.

30. Fairchild, 1896: 220-222, 1898; see Strong, 1895; Laidlaw, 1898, 1911; Taylor, 1899; Batten, 1903, 1908--as other examples. Laidlaw provides a valuable illustration of the complexity of the religion-reform-science intertwine. He was an active Methodist minister, a city-church reformer, and a researcher. His interest in research was to create an effective reform ministry to enlarge the work of the church. In the process he created **census tracts**. Would anyone today argue that their use represents an invasion of religious reform upon scientific research? Or, that census data was "unscientific" because it had

an applied orientation? (see Green, 1954: 46).

31. See Durkheim, 1919; Wallace, 1977.

VI

RECONSTRUCTING THE SOCIOLOGICAL PAST IN AMERICA

1. Bolce, 1909a,b,c; see Earp, 1915.

2. Leuba, 1916; see Oberschall, 1972.

3. Howerath, 1894.

4. Tolman, 1902-04.

5. The Bernard data remain largely unpublished, archived at the University of Chicago and Penn State. The small exception is Baker, 1973. Two unpublished papers have treated this material: Baker, et al., 1973; and Henking, 1984. My report is based primarily on the latter.

6. Veysey, 1965: 300-302.

7. This includes Ward, 1894, 1896; Giddings, 1893; Patten, 1894a,b; Small, 1895c; also see Giddings, 1896. Giddings is dealt with very little in this essay, primarily because he failed to get caught up in the Christian Sociology fray. He followed Sumner as president of the Society, and his chair in sociology at Columbia followed Small's at Chicago. Although he earned only a bachelor's degree, his department in the early years was next only to Chicago in doctorates conferred. He taught seminarians at Union (New York) from time to time but seems to have maintained an independence from the conflicts and pressures that surrounded Small. By and large, it was his students who filled in the gap between the Chicago school and Parsons (see Reed, 1982; Fine, 1979; Hinkle, 1980).

8. Small, 1916: 796-797.

9. Shaskolsky, 1970.

10. Schwendinger & Schwendinger, 1974; see Friedrichs, 1970.

11. See Durkheim, 1919, 1956; Wallace, 1975; Giddens, 1972.

12. See Friedrichs, 1970; Johnson, 1977.

13. Perrin, 1973, 1976.

14. See Schwendinger & Schwendinger, 1974; Faris, 1970; Baker, 1973.

15. See Friedrichs, 1970: 12-13. To THE STRUCTURE OF SOCIAL ACTION must also be added the early essays "The Role of Theory in Social Research" read in 1937 and "The Place of Ultimate Values in Sociological Theory" published in 1935 (Parsons, 1982: 65-92).

16. Parsons' phrase at the time of his retirement (see Reinhold, 1973: 80) was that he acted "as an importer," focusing attention on Weber and Durkheim. He contrasts their tendency to think in grand theoretical terms with the previous American inclination toward more narrow empirical studies. Whatever one may think of the merits of early American sociology, it was Parsons much more than Weber or Durkheim who drew the line between grand theory and empiricism (also see Parsons, 1959). Of course, both Durkheim and Weber were known in American sociological circles before Parsons, and each had visited the United States to give a paper. In fact, American sociology was very fond of European thinkers, and their work appeared regularly here in translation in the journals (see, e.g., Simmel, 1905). Intentionally or not, Parsons capitalized upon this interest and orienta-

72

tion in his own work, giving an overarching structure to some vague and undifferentiated underlying sensibilities. When I say, then, that Parsons "gave us Durkheim and Weber," I mean also that he ruled out a series of other potential sources.

17. In an essay developed towards the end of his career, Parsons (1977: 48) argued--with his own relative hegemony now established--that his "generalized media of exchange" or pattern variables were restatements and extensions of Thomas' four wishes plus the definition-of-the-situation concept. He did not expand upon this point in detail. It is one of the relatively few times that Parsons ties his work positively to earlier American sociology.

REFERENCES*

Ahlstrom, Sydney E. 1972. A RELIGIOUS HISTORY OF THE AMERICAN PEOPLE. New Haven: Yale.

ANNALS. 1893. "The American Institute of Christian Sociology," ANNALS OF THE AMERICAN ACADEMY OF POLITICAL AND SOCIAL SCIENCE 4: 491.

_____. 1895. "Associations." ANNALS ... 6: 182-184.

Arjomand, Said Amir. 1892. "A la recherche de la conscience collective." THE AMERICAN SOCIOLOGIST 17: 94-102.

Baker, Paul J. 1973. "The life histories of W.I. Thomas and Robert E. Park." AJS 79: 243-261.

Baker, Paul J., Martha P. Long, and Susan L. Quensel. 1973. "The pioneers of American sociology." Unpublished paper presented at the annual meeting of the American Sociological Association.

Barker, Eileen. 1981. "Science as theology," pp. 262-280 in A.R. Peacocke (ed.), THE SCIENCES AND THEOLOGY IN THE TWENTIETH CENTURY. Notre Dame, Indiana: University of Notre Dame.

Barnard, John. 1969. FROM EVANGELICALISM TO PROGRESSIVISM AT OBERLIN COLLEGE. n.p.: Ohio State University Press.

---

*AJS throughout refers to the AMERICAN JOURNAL OF SOCIOLOGY.

Barnes, Harry Elmer. 1926. "The place of Albion Wood-bury Small in modern sociology." AJS 32: 15-44.

_____. 1929. THE TWILIGHT OF CHRISTIANITY. New York: Vanguard.

Batten, Samuel Zane. 1903. "The church as the maker of conscience." AJS 7: 511-623.

_____. 1908. "The redemption of the unfit." AJS 14: 223-260.

Becker, Ernest. 1971. THE LOST SCIENCE OF MAN. New York: Braziller.

Berger, Peter L. 1963. INVITATION TO SOCIOLOGY. Garden City, N.Y.: Doubleday/Anchor.

_____. 1969. THE SACRED CANOPY. Garden City, N.Y.: Doubleday/Anchor.

Bernard, L.L. and Jessie Bernard. 1943. ORIGINS OF AMERICAN SOCIOLOGY. New York: Crowell.

Bierstedt, Robert. 1981. AMERICAN SOCIOLOGICAL THEORY. New York: Academic.

Bolce, Harold. 1909a. "Blasting at the rock of ages." COSMOPOLITAN 46: 665-676.

_____. 1909b. "Polyglots in the temple of Babylon." COSMOPOLITAN 47: 52-65.

_____. 1909c. "Avatars of the almighty." COSMOPOLITAN 47: 209-218.

Carey, James T. 1975. SOCIOLOGY AND PUBLIC AFFAIRS. Beverly HIlls, Calif.: Sage.

Cavanaugh, Michael A. 1982. "Pagan and Christian."

SOCIOLOGICAL ANALYSIS 43: 109-129.

Christakes, George. 1978. ALBION W. SMALL. Boston: Twayne.

Chugerman, Samuel. 1939. LESTER F. WARD. Durham, N.C.: Duke University.

Clow, F.R. 1920. "Sociology in normal schools." AJS 25: 584-636.

Commons, John R. 1892. "A popular bibliography of sociology." OBERLIN COLLEGE LIBRARY BULLETIN 1: 1-15.

_____. 1894. SOCIAL REFORM AND THE CHURCH. New York: Crowell.

_____. 1934. MYSELF. New York: Macmillan.

Crafts, Wilbur F. 1907. PRACTICAL CHRISTIAN SOCIOLOGY. New York: Funk & Wagnalls.

Curtis, Bruce. 1981. WILLIAM GRAHAM SUMNER. Boston: Twayne.

Davis, Rollin and Robert G. Perrin. 1982. "The Sociologist, 1883-1888." THE SOUTHERN SOCIOLOGIST 14 (2): 28.

Dealey, James Quayle. 1927. "Lester Frank Ward," pp. 61-96 in Howard W. Odum (ed.), AMERICAN MASTERS OF SOCIAL SCIENCE. New York: Holt.

Dibble, Vernon K. 1975. THE LEGACY OF ALBION SMALL. Chicago: University of Chicago.

Dombrowski, James. 1936. THE EARLY DAYS OF CHRISTIAN SOCIALISM IN AMERICA. New York: Columbia University.

Dressner, Richard B. 1972. CHRISTIAN SOCIALISM. Unpublished Ph.D. dissertation, Cornell University.

Durkheim, Emile. 1919. "The school of tomorrow," pp. 185-192 in Ferdinand Buisson and Frederic E. Farrington (eds.), FRENCH EDUCATIONAL IDEALS OF TODAY. New York: World.

_____. 1956. EDUCATION AND SOCIOLOGY. Glencoe, Illinois: Free Press.

Dynes, Russell R. 1974. "Sociology as a religious movement." THE AMERICAN SOCIOLOGIST 9: 169-176.

Earp, Edwin L. 1915. Comments on Henry Prichett: "Reasonable restrictions upon the scholar's freedom." PAPERS AND PROCEEDINGS OF THE NINTH ANNUAL MEETING OF THE AMERICAN SOCIOLOGICAL SOCIETY: 166-167.

Ellwood, Charles A. 1910. "The psychological view of society." AJS 15: 596-610.

_____. 1913. "The social function of religion." AJS 19: 289-307.

_____. 1920. "Religion and democracy." PAPERS AND PROCEEDINGS OF THE FOURTEENTH ANNUAL MEETING OF THE AMERICAN SOCIOLOGICAL SOCIETY: 127-133.

_____. 1922. THE RECONSTRUCTION OF RELIGION. New York: Macmillan.

_____. 1923. CHRISTIANITY AND SOCIAL SCIENCE. New York: Macmillan.

Ely, Richard T. 1889a. AN INTRODUCTION TO POLITICAL ECONOMY. New York: Chautauqua Press.

_____. 1889b. SOCIAL ASPECTS OF CHRISTIANITY. New York: Crowell.

_____. 1894. SOCIALISM AND SOCIAL REFORM. New York: Crowell.

_____. 1896. THE SOCIAL LAW OF SERVICE. New York: Eaton & Mains.

_____. 1938. GROUND UNDER OUR FEET. New York: Macmillan.

Evangelical Alliance for the United States. 1894. CHRISTIANITY PRACTICALLY APPLIED. New York: Baker & Taylor.

Fairchild, E.M. 1896. "The function of the church." AJS 2: 220-233.

_____. 1898. "Ethical instruction in school and church." AJS 4: 433-447.

Faris, Robert E.L. 1970. CHICAGO SOCIOLOGY. Chicago: University of Chicago.

Fine, William F. 1979. PROGRESSIVE EVOLUTIONISM AND AMERICAN SOCIOLOGY. n.p.: UMI Research Press.

Friedrichs, Robert W. 1970. A SOCIOLOGY OF SOCIOLOGY. New York: Free Press.

Fuhrman, Ellsworth R. 1978. "Images of the discipline in early American sociology." JOURNAL OF THE HISTORY OF SOCIOLOGY 1: 81-116.

_____. 1980. THE SOCIOLOGY OF KNOWLEDGE IN AMERICA. Charlottesville: University Press of Virginia.

Fukuyama, Yoshio. 1963. "The uses of sociology." JOURNAL FOR THE SCIENTIFIC STUDY OF RELIGION 2: 195-203.

Furner, Mary O. 1975. ADVOCACY & OBJECTIVITY. Lexington: University Press of Kentucky.

Gerver, Israel. 1963. LESTER FRANK WARD. New York: Crowell.

Giddens, Anthony. 1972. POLITICS AND SOCIOLOGY IN THE THOUGHT OF MAX WEBER. London: Macmillan.

Giddings, Franklin H. 1893. THE THEORY OF SOCIOLOGY. Philadelphia: American Academy of Political and Social Science.

_____. 1896. PRINCIPLES OF SOCIOLOGY. New York: Macmillan.

Goodspeed, Thomas W. 1926. "Albion W. Small." AJS 32: 1-14.

Green, Howard Whipple. 1954. "Serving the urban community," pp. 43-50 in Robert A. McKibben (ed.), METHODISM LOOKS AT THE CITY. New York: Division of National Missions/Board of Missions--The Methodist Church.

Hadden, Jeffrey K., Charles Longino, and Myer S. Reed, Jr. 1974. "Further reflections on the development of sociology and the social gospel in America." SOCIOLOGICAL ANALYSIS 35: 282-286.

Harter, Lafayette G., Jr. 1962. JOHN R. COMMONS. Corvallis: Oregon State University.

Henderson, Charles R. 1895. "Sociology and theology," AJS 1: 381-383.

Henking, Susan E. 1984. "American protestantism and

American sociology." Unpublished paper presented at a special session on "Sociology and Christianity" presented at the annual meeting of the American Sociological Association.

HERALD, 1894a. "The summer school." The Grinnell HERALD 27 (June 29): 2.

_____. 1894b. "The summer school." The Grinnell HERALD 27 (July 3): 2.

_____. 1894c. "The summer school." The Grinnell HERALD 27 (July 6): 2.

Herron, George D. 1894. THE CHRISTIAN SOCIETY. New York: Revell.

_____. 1895. THE CHRISTIAN STATE. New York: Revell.

Hinkle, Roscoe C. 1980. FOUNDING THEORY OF AMERICAN SOCIOLOGY. Boston: Routledge & Kegan Paul.

Hinkle, Roscoe C. and Gisela J. Hinkle. 1954. THE DEVELOPMENT OF MODERN SOCIOLOGY. New York: Random House.

Holbrook, Z. Swift. 1892. THE LESSONS OF THE HOMESTEAD TROUBLES. Chicago: Knight, Leonard.

_____. 1894. "Christian sociology." BIBLIOTHECA SACRA 51: 537-559.

_____. 1895a. "What is sociology." BIBLIOTHECA SACRA 52: 458-504.

_____. 1895b. "Professor Herron's impressionism." BIBLIOTHECA SACRA 52: 561-563.

_____. 1896. "Christian sociology again." BIBLIOTHECA

SACRA 53: 171-173.

Howerath, Ira W. 1894. "Present condition of sociology in the United States." ANNALS ... 5: 260-269.

Janowitz, Morris. 1972. "Professionalization of sociology." AJS 78: 105-135.

Johnson, Benton. 1977. "Sociological theory and religious truth." SOCIOLOGICAL ANALYSIS 38: 368-388.

Jones, Peter D'A. 1968. THE CHRISTIAN SOCIALIST REVIVAL. Princeton: Princeton University.

Laidlaw, Walter. 1898. "A plea and plan for a co-operative church parish system in cities." AJS 3: 795-808.

_____. 1911. "The church and the city community." AJS 16: 794-804.

Lazarsfeld, Paul F. 1962. "The sociology of empirical social research." AMERICAN SOCIOLOGICAL REVIEW 27: 757-767.

Leuba, James H. 1916. BELIEF IN GOD AND IMMORTALITY. Boston: Sherman, French.

Lyon, David. 1983. "The idea of a Christian sociology." SOCIOLOGICAL ANALYSIS 44: 227-242.

McClosky, Robert Green. 1951. AMERICAN CONSERVATISM IN THE AGE OF ENTERPRISE. New York: Harper & Row.

MacCunn, John. 1907. SIX RADICAL THINKERS. London: Arnold.

Martindale, Don. 1960. THE NATURE AND TYPES OF SOCIOLOGICAL THEORY. Boston: Houghton Mifflin.

Mathews, Shailer. 1895. "Christian sociology." AJS 1: 69-78.

_____. 1895-96. "Christian sociology [series]." AJS: 1: 182-194, 359-380, 457-472, 604-617, 771-784; 2: 108-117, 274-287, 416-432.

_____. 1899a. "The significance of the church to the social movement." AJS 4: 603-620.

_____. 1899b. "The Christian church and social unity." AJS 5: 456-469.

_____. 1910. THE SOCIAL GOSPEL. Philadelphia: Griffith & Rowland.

_____. 1912. "The social origin of theology." AJS 18: 289-317.

_____. 1936. NEW FAITH FOR OLD. New York: Macmillan.

Mills, C. Wright. 1943. "The professional ideology of social pathologists." AJS 49: 165-180.

Morgan, J. Graham. 1969. "The development of sociology and the social gospel in America." SOCIOLOGICAL ANALYSIS 30: 42-53.

Mott, Frank Luther. 1938. A HISTORY OF AMERICAN MAGAZINES. Cambridge: Harvard University.

Oberschall, Anthony. 1972. "The institutionalization of American sociology," pp. 187-251 in Anthony Oberschall (ed.), THE ESTABLISHMENT OF EMPIRICAL SOCIOLOGY. New York: Harper & Row.

O'Connor, WIlliam T. 1942. NATURALISM AND THE PIONEERS OF AMERICAN SOCIOLOGY. Washington, D.C.: Catholic University.

OUTLOOK. 1893. "An American institute of Christian sociology." OUTLOOK 48: 134-135.

Page, Charles Hunt. 1940. CLASS AND AMERICAN SOCIOLOGY. New York: Dial.

Parsons, Talcott. 1937. THE STRUCTURE OF SOCIAL ACTION. New York: McGraw-Hill.

_____. 1959. "A short account of my intellectual development." ALPHA KAPPA DELTAN 29: 3-12.

_____. 1977. SOCIAL SYSTEMS AND THE EVOLUTION OF ACTION THEORY. New York: Free Press.

_____. 1982. ON INSTITUTIONS AND SOCIAL EVOLUTION. Chicago: University of Chicago.

Patten, Simon N. 1894a. "The failure of biologic sociology." ANNALS ... 4: 919-947.

_____. 1894b. "The organic concept of society." ANNALS ... 5: 404-409.

_____. 1911. THE SOCIAL BASIS OF RELIGION. New York: Macmillan.

Perrin, Robert C. 1973. "The functionalist theory of change revisited." PACIFIC SOCIOLOGICAL REVIEW 16: 47-60.

_____. 1976. "Herbert Spencer's four theories of social evolution." AJS 81: 1338-1359.

Poloma, Margaret. 1982. "Toward a Christian sociological perspective." SOCIOLOGICAL ANALYSIS 42: 95-108.

Rader, Benjamin G. 1966. THE ACADEMIC MIND AND REFORM. Lexington: University of Kentucky.

Rauschenbusch, Walter. 1896. "The ideals of social reformers." AJS 2: 202-219.

_____. 1897. "The stake of the church in the social movement." AJS 3: 18-30.

_____. 1907. CHRISTIANITY AND THE SOCIAL CRISIS. New York: Association.

Reed, Myer S., Jr. 1975. DIFFERENTIATION AND DEVELOPMENT IN A SCIENTIFIC SPECIALITY. Unpublished Ph.D. dissertation, Tulane University.

_____. 1981. "An alliance for progress." SOCIOLOGICAL ANALYSIS 42: 27-46.

_____. 1982. "After the alliance." SOCIOLOGICAL ANALYSIS 42: 189-204.

Reinhold, Robert. 1973. "A mentor of sociologists retires after 42 years at Harvard post." New York TIMES (June 14): 49, 80.

REVIEW. 1984. "The church in society." REVIEW OF REVIEWS 9: 748-749.

Rosenberg, Bernard. 1963. THORSTEIN VEBLEN. New York: Crowell.

Ross, Edward Alsworth. 1895-1900. "Social control [series]." AJS 1: 513-535, 753-770; 2: 92-107, 255-263, 433-445, 547-566, 823-838; 3: 64-78, 236-247, 328-339, 502-519, 649-661, 809-828; 5: 475-487, 604-616, 761-777; 6: 29-41, 238-247, 381-395, 550-562.

_____. 1897. "The educational function of the church." OUTLOOK 15: 1936-1940.

_____. 1901. SOCIAL CONTROL. New York: Macmillan.

_____. 1907. SIN AND SOCIETY. New York: Macmillan.

_____. 1920. Discussion of Charles A. Ellwood: "Religion and democracy." PAPERS AND PROCEEDINGS OF THE FOURTEENTH ANNUAL MEETING OF THE AMERICAN SOCIOLOGICAL SOCIETY: 133-134.

_____. 1936. SEVENTY YEARS OF IT. New York: Appleton.

SCARLET AND BLACK. 1894. "The summer school." SCARLET AND BLACK (Sept. 12): 1.

Schwendinger, Herman and Julia R. Schwendinger. 1974. SOCIOLOGISTS OF THE CHAIR. New York: Basic Books.

Scott, Clifford. 1976. LESTER FRANK WARD. Boston: Twayne.

Shaskolsky, Leon. 1970. "The development of sociological theory in America," pp. 6-30 in Larry T. Reynolds and Janice M. Reynolds (eds.), THE SOCIOLOGY OF SOCIOLOGY. New York: McKay.

Shils, Edward. 1948. THE PRESENT STATE OF AMERICAN SOCIOLOGY. Glencoe, Illinois: Free Press.

Simmel, Georg. 1905. "A contribution to the sociology of religion." AJS 11: 359-376.

Singer, Anna M. 1926. WALTER RAUSCHENBUSCH AND HIS CONTRIBUTION TO SOCIAL CHRISITIANITY. Boston: Badger.

Small, Albion W. 1890. INTRODUCTION TO A SCIENCE OF SOCIETY. Waterville, Maine: Colby University.

_____. 1895a. "The era of sociology." AJS 1: 1-15.

_____. 1895b. "Methods of studying society." THE CHAU-
TAUQUAN 21: 52-56.

_____. 1895c. "The organic concept of society." ANNALS
... 5: 740-746.

_____. 1897a. "The sociologists' point of view." AJS
3: 145-170.

_____. 1897b. "The meaning of the social movement."
AJS 3: 340-354.

_____. 1901. "The church and the social problem."
INDEPENDENT 53: 537-539.

_____. 1905. GENERAL SOCIOLOGY. Chicago: Univer-
sity of Chicago.

_____. 1906. Review of Louis O. Wallis, EGOISM. AJS
11: 848-849.

_____. 1907. ADAM SMITH AND MODERN SOCIOLOGY.
Chicago: University of Chicago.

_____. 1909. THE CAMERALISTS. Chicago: University
of Chicago.

_____. 1910. THE MEANING OF SOCIAL SCIENCE.
Chicago: University of Chicago.

_____. 1916. "Fifty years of sociology in the United
States." AJS 21: 721-864.

_____. 1920. "Christianity and industry." AJS 25: 673-694.

_____. 1924. ORIGINS OF SOCIOLOGY. Chicago: Univer-
sity of Chicago.

Small, Albion W. and George E. Vincent. 1894. INTRO-
DUCTION TO THE STUDY OF SOCIETY. New York:
American Book Company.

Smith, Dusky Lee. 1970. "Sociology and the rise of corporate capitalism," pp. 68-84 in Larry T. Reynolds and Janice M. Reynolds (eds.), THE SOCIOLOGY OF SOCIOLOGY. New York: McKay.

Spencer, Herbert. 1929. THE STUDY OF SOCIOLOGY. New York: Appleton.

Starr, Harris E. 1925. WILLIAM GRAHAM SUMNER. New York: Holt.

Stern, Bernhard J. 1933. "The letters of Albion W. Small to Lester F. Ward." SOCIAL FORCES 12: 163-173.

_____. 1935. YOUNG WARD'S DIARY. New York: Putnams.

Stuckenberg, J.H.W. 1880. CHRISTIAN SOCIOLOGY. New York: Funk.

_____. 1885. THE FINAL SCIENCE. New York: Funk & Wagnalls.

_____. 1893. THE AGE AND THE CHURCH. Hartford, Connecticut: Student.

_____. 1898. INTRODUCTION TO THE STUDY OF SOCIOLOGY. New York: Armstrong.

_____. 1903. SOCIOLOGY. New York: Putnams.

Sumner, William Graham. 1910. "Religion and the mores." AJS 15: 577-591.

Swatos, William H., Jr. 1980. "Five more years." THE SOUTHERN SOCIOLOGIST 11 (2): 15-18.

_____. 1983. "The faith of the fathers." SOCIOLOGICAL ANALYSIS 44: 37-52.

Taylor, Graham. 1899. "The social function of the church." AJS 5: 305-321.

_____. 1930. PIONEERING ON SOCIAL FRONTIERS. Chicago: University of Chicago.

Tillich, Paul J. 1938. "Protestantism in the present world situation." AJS 43: 236-248.

Tolman, Frank. 1902-04. "The study of sociology in institutions of higher learning in the United States [series]." AJS 7: 797-838; 8: 85-121, 251-272, 531-538.

Veysey, Laurence R. 1965. THE EMERGENCE OF THE AMERICAN UNIVERSITY. Chicago: University of Chicago.

Voegelin, Eric. 1952. THE NEW SCIENCE OF POLITICS. Chicago: University of Chicago.

Vree, Dale. 1976. ON SYNTHESIZING MARXISM AND CHRISTIANITY. New York: Wiley.

Wade, Louise C. 1964. GRAHAM TAYLOR. Chicago: University of Chicago.

Wallace, Ruth. 1977. "Emile Durkheim and the civil religion concept." REVIEW OF RELIGIOUS RESEARCH 18: 287-290.

Wallis, Louis O. 1903. "The capitalization of social development." AJS 7: 763-796.

_____. 1905. EGOISM. Chicago: University of Chicago.

_____. 1907a. "Sociological significance of the Bible." AJS 12: 532-552.

_____. 1907b. "Sociology and theism." AJS 12: 838-844.

_____. 1908-11. "Biblical sociology [series]." AJS 14: 145-170, 306-328, 497-533; 15: 214-243; 16: 392-419; 17: 61-76, 329-350.

_____. 1912. SOCIOLOGICAL STUDY OF THE BIBLE. Chicago: University of Chicago.

Ward, Lester F. 1883. DYNAMIC SOCIOLOGY. New York: Appleton.

_____. 1892. PSYCHIC FACTORS IN CIVILIZATION. Boston: Ginn.

_____. 1895. "The place of sociology among the sciences." AJS 1: 16-27.

_____. 1913-18. GILMPSES OF THE COSMOS. New York: Putnams.

Weber, Max. 1958. "Science as a vocation," pp. 129 to 156 in H.H. Gerth and C. Wright Mills (eds.), FROM MAX WEBER. New York: Oxford.

Weinberg, Julius. 1972. EDWARD ALSWORTH ROSS. Madison: State Historical Society of Wisconsin.

Westby, David L. 1958. Book review essay. JOURNAL OF THE HISTORY OF SOCIOLOGY 1: 120-131.

Williams, Robin M., Jr. 1976. "Sociology in America," pp. 77-111 in Charles M. Bonjean, Louis Schneider, and Robert L. Lineberry (eds.), SOCIAL SCIENCE IN AMERICA. Austin: University of Texas.

Wolff, Kurt H. 1946. "Notes toward a sociocultural interpretation of American sociology." AMERICAN SOCIOLOGICAL REVIEW 11: 545-553.

Woodward, C.M. 1887. THE MANUAL TRAINING

SCHOOL. Boston: Heath.

Wright, G. Frederick. 1916. STORY OF MY LIFE AND WORK. Oberlin: Bibliotheca Sacra.

Young, Martin L. 1896. "Some reasons why a minister should study sociology." LUTHERAN QUARTERLY 26: 365-374.

Youmans, E.L. and W.J. Youmans. 1880. "Sociology and theology at Yale College." POPULAR SCIENCE MONTHLY 17: 265-269.

ABOUT THE AUTHOR

Like William Graham Sumner but 106 years later, William H. Swatos, Jr., was born in Paterson, New Jersey, A century after Sumner was instituted as rector of his first (and only) parish, the author was also ordained to the Episcopalian priesthood, having completed undergraduate studies with honors in sociology at Transylvania University in Lexington, Kentucky, a Master of Divinity degree **summa cum laude** from the Episcopal Theological Seminary in Kentucky, and concurrently a Master of Arts in sociology from the University of Kentucky. He received the doctorate in sociology from the same university in 1973, writing a dissertation applying church-sect theory to the transfer of the Anglican episcopate from the British isles to the western hemisphere that was subsequently published by the Society for the Scientific Study of Religion as INTO DENOMINATIONALISM: THE ANGLICAN METAMORPHOSIS. From then 'til 1980 he taught and was chairman of the department of sociology at King College in Bristol, Tennessee, where like John Commons, he eventually had his chair pulled out from under him. Since that time--with the exception of a sojourn as Fulbright Lecturer on the Faculty of Theology at the University of Iceland--he has been Vicar of St. Mark's Episcopal Church in Silvis, Diocese of Quincy, Illinois. In 1983 he was appointed Visiting Lecturer in sociology at Augustana College, Rock Island, Illinois, and in 1984 Lecturer in sociology at Northern Illinois University, DeKalb, Illinois. Dr. Swatos is a member of the Executive Council of the Association for the Sociology of Religion and serves on the staff of its journal, SOCIOLOGICAL ANALYSIS. He is also an associate editor of the REVIEW OF RELIGIOUS RESEARCH.

INDEX

11 029